CONTENTS

Chapter One: Crime and Violence

Does Britain need fixing?	1
Violence in street crime	4
The right to fight	5
Fear of crime or anxiety about a changing society?	6
Weapons and the law	7
Anti-social behaviour	8

Chapter Two: Youth Crime

Police 'should break up gangs'	9
Coping with kidulthood	11
Gang membership	12
Get rid of 'gangs'	14
Gun and knife crime survey	15
Youth justice	16
Too young to be a criminal	19
Young people, crime and public perceptions	20
The fear of young people damages us all	22

Chapter Three: Dealing with Crime

Engaging communities in fighting crime	23
Crime, sentencing and your community	24
Community sentencing	27
More offenders serve community punishments	28
Offenders to wear high-visibility jackets	28
Going ballistic	29
Restorative justice	31
The danger of Tasers	31
Thousands of new Tasers for the police	32
'Reclaim the streets' plea by new think-tank report	33
Stop and search	34
Rights on arrest	35
How ASBOs help	36
Prison sentences 'too soft'	37
More knife crime offenders jailed	38
Prison – why should I care?	39

Key Facts	40
Glossary	41
Index	42
Additional Resources	43
Acknowledgements	44

Useful information for readers

Dear Reader,

Issues: Crime in the UK

Media reports concerning violent crime and the rhetoric of "Broken Britain" are now worryingly familiar, but just how serious is the UK's crime problem? This books examines different types of crime and how they can best be tackled. **Crime in the UK** also looks at types of crime particularly associated with young people, and whether this group is unfairly blamed for much crime in our society.

The purpose of *Issues*

Crime in the UK is the one hundred and seventy-seventh volume in the **Issues** series. The aim of this series is to offer up-to-date information about important issues in our world. Whether you are a regular reader or new to the series, we do hope you find this book a useful overview of the many and complex issues involved in the topic. This title replaces an older volume in the **Issues** series, Volume 137: **Crime and Anti-Social Behaviour**, which is now out of print.

Titles in the **Issues** series are resource books designed to be of especial use to those undertaking project work or requiring an overview of facts, opinions and information on a particular subject, particularly as a prelude to undertaking their own research.

The information in this book is not from a single author, publication or organisation; the value of this unique series lies in the fact that it presents information from a wide variety of sources, including:

⇨ Government reports and statistics
⇨ Newspaper articles and features
⇨ Information from think-tanks and policy institutes
⇨ Magazine features and surveys
⇨ Website material
⇨ Literature from lobby groups and charitable organisations.*

Critical evaluation

Because the information reprinted here is from a number of different sources, readers should bear in mind the origin of the text and whether the source is likely to have a particular bias or agenda when presenting information (just as they would if undertaking their own research). It is hoped that, as you read about the many aspects of the issues explored in this book, you will critically evaluate the information presented. It is important that you decide whether you are being presented with facts or opinions. Does the writer give a biased or an unbiased report? If an opinion is being expressed, do you agree with the writer?

Crime in the UK offers a useful starting point for those who need convenient access to information about the many issues involved. However, it is only a starting point. Following each article is a URL to the relevant organisation's website, which you may wish to visit for further information.

Kind regards,

Lisa Firth
Editor, **Issues** series

** Please note that Independence Publishers has no political affiliations or opinions on the topics covered in the **Issues** series, and any views quoted in this book are not necessarily those of the publisher or its staff.*

Does Britain need fixing?

Britain is not broken, but parts of it are severely dysfunctional, despite the high social spending of the past decade. And, thanks to the distorting lens of the media and the strange psychology of risk, the public thinks the problems are worse than they are

Imagine a country where virtually everyone describes themselves as satisfied with their lives – only 13 per cent say they are unhappy. Where 95 per cent say they are close to their families and 76 per cent are confident about their personal futures. A country that is markedly better off than a decade before, with 600,000 fewer people in poverty and one million fewer on out-of-work benefits. A country with universal free healthcare and the highest recorded level of satisfaction with that service, with waiting times the lowest for 40 years. A country which most people think is a good place to raise children and where most children are felt to have far better prospects than their parents had before them. But in that same country, when asked whether life in general is getting better or worse, 71 per cent of people say life is getting worse, up from 60 per cent in 2007 and only 40 per cent in 1998.

This country is, of course, Britain. Last September, David Cameron, the man most likely to be its next prime minister, said: 'The biggest challenge facing Britain today is mending our broken society...Four in every five youngsters receiving custodial sentences have no qualifications. More than two-thirds of prisoners are illiterate. And nearly one-third of those excluded from school have been involved with substance abuse...43 per cent of 11 year olds cannot read, write and add up properly. Last month, more than 20,000 pupils left school without a GCSE. And right now, more than a million young people are not in education, work or training.'

The Conservatives have made much of this 'broken Britain' narrative. But what does it actually amount to? Strip

By Ben Page, chairman of the Ipsos MORI Social Research Institute

away the rhetoric, and you find three basic claims: crime and anti-social behaviour are rampant; the institution of the family is in dangerous decline; and there is a growing underclass of poorly educated, 'feral' young people.

A sense of proportion

Take the first of these – crime and anti-social behaviour. Iain Duncan Smith's Centre for Social Justice's critique of Britain – which informs much of Cameron's 'broken society' thinking – provides a long list of social ills. Duncan Smith's report, published in 2006, drew upon international league tables to paint a bleak picture of modern Britain. British teenagers, we were told, drank more, learned less, had sex earlier and were more likely to suffer mental illness than their counterparts in most other European countries.

This certainly chimes with the bleak narrative we see in much of the media of a modern Britain riven by crime and disorder. The newspapers tell a story of binge drinking, family breakdown, gang culture, consumerism, the decline of small shops, violence, the sexualisation of young girls, workaholism, over-examination in schools, inadequate childcare, a paralysis in social mobility, ingrained pockets of deprivation, junk food, solitary screen-based entertainment and celebrity culture.

Consider violent youth crime, one of the hot-button issues of recent years. No one doubts that there is a serious problem in some parts of the

country. Teenage killings in London have risen from 15 in 2006 to 27 in 2007, and stood at 21 halfway through 2008. But to read the *Daily Mail*, one of the government's chief tormentors, is to encounter a Britain apparently on the brink of bloody collapse. Take this lurid piece, from 20 July: 'A few nights ago, as an 18-year-old stab victim lay in a pool of blood awaiting his statistical turn to become the 21st teenager to die violently in the streets of London this year, we learned that crime statistics are dropping dramatically. All is well. Home Secretary Jacqui Smith, while concerned that "knives are still being used", is best pleased. As well she might be, for the figures are the creation of none other than the British Crime Survey, itself a creation of Jacqui's Home Office. If the British Crime Survey sounds like a vast analytical

laboratory stuffed with academics in some ivy-clad university city, that is the whole idea.'

As that quote suggests, public trust in official statistics has fallen sharply in Britain in the last decade, as public service 'delivery' has moved to the centre of political argument. This actually began when Margaret Thatcher made over 20 revisions to ways in which unemployment was counted in the 1980s. But today the political dispute over social data makes it harder for a neutral observer to reach a balanced view.

Overall crime rates have fallen by around 40 per cent over the past decade. Violent crime has, however, failed to fall as quickly as other crime

---

According to the mistrusted British Crime Survey (a big annual survey of experience of crime involving about 40,000 respondents), overall crime rates have fallen by around 40 per cent over the past decade. Violent crime has, however, failed to fall as quickly as other crime, according to the BCS, while violent offences recorded by the police – the other way of measuring crime – have actually increased since 2001, and weapons offences by almost 40 per cent. This may help account for the public's ever-rising fear of crime, which is otherwise hard to explain, given the 70 per cent increase in police spending in the last ten years, the raising of police numbers to their highest level ever and the imprisonment of 20,000 more criminals – let alone the plunge in the official crime numbers.

Perhaps we just need a sense of perspective on our own pessimism. Although Britons are more negative than many other countries, our levels of what the former government adviser Roger Liddle calls 'social pessimism' are more than matched in some of the big EU states. Liddle's analysis (see his essay *Social Pessimism: The New Social Reality of Europe*, www. policy-network.net), undertaken for

European commission president José Manuel Barroso, is based on the latest Eurobarometer survey, which asks people whether they believe their lives will be better in 20 years. Many smaller countries, like Estonia (78 per cent) and Ireland (67 per cent), are optimistic, but citizens of the EU's big four feel less good about the future: in Britain just 36 per cent are optimistic, in France 27 per cent, in Germany 20 per cent and in Italy 32 per cent.

What's broken, and what isn't?

If the broken Britain hypothesis were true, one would expect to find clear evidence for it across a range of social indicators and in measurements of self-declared wellbeing. But the picture is not so clear-cut. It is true that 60 per cent of us say we would like Britain to be more like it used to be, a significant rise from 37 per cent in 1999. Yet the proportion of Britons describing themselves as happy with their own lives has changed relatively little. Either Britain has always been broken (or never was), or the 'brokenness' has little bearing on personal wellbeing – which seems unlikely. As I noted at the beginning of this article, most people (87 per cent) say they are satisfied with their lives, and the proportion saying they are very satisfied is well ahead of that in many other large European nations. Despite our unusually acute anxieties about crime and disorder, we are simply not that miserable.

Moreover, looking at another of the three central claims of the broken Britain hypothesis – that we are increasingly a nation of dysfunctional families – the picture remains messy. Most of us still believe that families and marriage matter. Eight out of ten of us think family matters more than friends. Most of us (56 per cent), including the young, believe marriage is very important, and this view is common across all classes. We also think (70 per cent) it is better for parents to be married. Most of us (57 per cent) are even happy for governments to encourage marriage.

On the other hand, we do not believe in staying together for the sake of the children – we are somewhat more likely to divorce than other Europeans (our rate is 15.6 per cent). Duncan Smith's report blames this on

a rise in cohabitation: 'The increase in family breakdown...is now driven entirely by the increase in unstable cohabiting partnerships.' Yet we are actually no more likely to cohabit than other nations – and less likely than the happier Danes and Swedes, as well as the French and Germans.

We do, however, have more teenagers living in single-parent families – just over one in ten. This is higher than any other European nation, but not by much; it is very similar to the Swedes and Danes and less than the god-fearing US. Nevertheless, as Anastasia de Waal explains in her book *Second Thoughts on the Family* (Civitas), in Britain, single parenthood is much more likely to be connected with poverty and instability than in Nordic countries (where marriage and cohabiting have become interchangeable). It is also true that we have one of the highest rates of teenage pregnancy in Europe, markedly higher than France or the Scandinavian countries. Yet it is worth noting that only just over two British 15 to 19 year olds out of 100 get pregnant.

What about the pathologies of the alleged teenage underclass? British teenagers do like a drink: they consume more alcohol than most other European young people, although not as much as in Ireland or Denmark, two of the happiest countries in Europe. Yet alcohol consumption among both teenagers and adults is now stable or in decline in Britain as public agencies devote more attention to the problem.

And drugs? Clearly they are a big part of the problems affecting some communities – but 80 per cent of teenagers in Britain never take them, and overall drug-taking among young people is also static or falling, as it is among adults. Do we have particularly violent young people? Well, 44 per cent of our 11 to 15 year olds say they have been involved in fights, but that is not the highest figure in Europe. And when we look at more generalised disorder and disrespect – a big concern of the public – the trends are again static or falling. Tony Blair's 'respect agenda' may not have made a big difference, popular with the public though it was, but outside particular hotspots, there is no evidence that our streets are getting worse. The fear spread by high-visibility 'signal' crimes, like knife crime in London, does, however, radiate out much further than the number of cases would warrant.

What really bothers the British

Britons' greatest concerns are centred around young people – both the safety of their own young, and fear of other, 'feral' young. Each English local authority surveys its residents every two years on quality of life, and the most common issue raised – far ahead of improvements to services like schools or hospitals – is facilities for teenagers. The more young people there are in a local authority, the more concerned the population will be about anti-social behaviour. As many as 84 per cent of us now agree that young people have too much freedom and need more discipline. Similarly, when you ask the British what educational issues concern them most, pupil behaviour and discipline comes out far ahead of attainment, exams, class sizes or anything else. It is possible to exaggerate this perceived 'crisis of authority' – we were already concerned about this problem a decade ago – but the situation is clearly not improving. We are also more worried about crime, especially youth crime, than any other Westerners, except the Dutch, and much more so than the Americans. Our feelings of safety are among the lowest in western Europe – only in former communist countries do people feel less safe.

When people are asked what would do most to address their number one concern, their most frequent answer is not more police on the beat, more criminals in jail or tougher sentences – but better parenting. Perhaps because of our historic individualism, the British seem to have weaker family ties than most European countries – for example, fewer children here eat regular meals with their parents. Maybe it is not so much the formal institution of marriage we need to look at, but the ways families, married or otherwise, work, and the ways we raise and look after our young people. (Although we are moving in a more continental direction, we still have a culture of family-unfriendly long working hours.)

Why people think Britain is broken

This brief balance sheet suggests that the claim that Britain as a whole is broken in any meaningful sense is hard to stand up. In the three areas of brokenness – crime and anti-social behaviour, family breakdown and the underclass – we are neither vastly out of step with other developed nations nor experiencing any massive increase in these problems.

Boris Johnson, the new Conservative mayor of London, recently poured scorn on the broken Britain claim. 'If you believe the politicians, we have a broken society, in which the courage and morals of young people have been sapped by welfarism and political correctness. And if you look at...the Beijing Olympics, you can see what piffle that is.' When in opposition, Tony Blair described Britain as 'unfit for any decent person to raise a family and live in'. But by the time he had been in power for a decade he had changed his mind. Blair now believes that the recent spate of murders of teenagers is 'not a metaphor for the state of British society', but a 'specific criminal culture among a specific group of people'.

The simple explanation for the apparent disagreement between the Conservative mayor and the Conservative leader, and the difference between post-1997 and pre-1997 Blair, is that one is in power and the other in opposition. Johnson and Cameron will no doubt find a way of blending their rhetoric to agree that parts of British society are broken. Indeed, in the Cameron 'broken society' speech quoted at the start of this piece, it is noticeable how much of the list refers to quite specific, often small-scale but very visible social pathologies. (The exception is educational attainment – although public concern about education is now at its lowest level for a decade.) It is also noticeable how many of the items on the broken Britain list are problems of excess and transgression, as opposed to the issues of deprivation, poverty and disease that characterised the 'the sick man of Europe' narrative about 1970s and 1980s Britain.

So why are we so much more pessimistic about Britain than the facts would seem to justify? One part of the answer is the British mass media – sometimes fanned by an aggressively adversarial party political system. Asked which institutions have the strongest impact on life in Britain, the public place the media before the government, parliament or the prime minister. And most people will agree that the media are responsible for the dark view they have of the country. Of course, people will agree with all sorts of propositions put to them in a survey, and journalists will tell us that the media are only reporting what happens. But ask people why they believe crime is rising, contrary to what most of the data shows, and only 23 per cent cite their own experience.

This helps to explain how most people are able to believe that crime or immigration or the NHS is not a big issue where they live, while simultaneously believing that the same issues are out of control in the country as a whole. MORI's weekly analysis of the coverage of street crime in London shows that perceptions of whether the capital as whole is getting more or less safe are strongly correlated with newspaper coverage of street crime, despite the fact that most Londoners feel safer walking around in their own neighbourhoods after dark than they used to.

So while most of us seem pretty content with our own lives, we are ready to go along with the collective pessimism. The economic downturn will only accentuate this phenomenon. And yet even with pessimism about the economy at record levels, when people focus on their own lives, a more balanced picture emerges. As recently as June, after a surge in concern about the economy, polls still found that more Britons felt their circumstances would improve over the next few years than felt they would get worse.

But the power of the media is only one part of the explanation for social pessimism – after all, those who never read a newspaper have similar views to those who do. Also, as the figures quoted earlier by Roger Liddle suggest, this is a Europe-wide phenomenon – and the media in other European countries are usually less aggressive and cynical than ours. So what else is going on? Notwithstanding the tendency to exaggerate social breakdown, there clearly are islands of social misery, made worse by the decline of traditional communities and authorities, especially in working-class areas. Liddle's own explanation is related to economic change: 'I believe that the erosion of "good working-class jobs" is having profound social effects both in Britain and on the continent. Not only are there material consequences for the groups affected. There is a loss of self-esteem, as the type of job which was in the previous generation the foundation of secure family life is no longer available. The alienation of white working-class males is not just a British phenomenon.'

Liddle also believes that the message of 'education, education, education' is threatening to families who have no history of success in formal education. 'In previous generations, people had routes, admittedly limited, from the shop floor into foreman and management positions. For young people today, obtaining educational qualifications is a necessary stepping stone for social mobility. We live in a world rich in educational opportunity, but the realisation that this is not one in which they are likely to succeed hits many young teenagers at secondary school – a fifth of whom across Europe leave school with no or very low qualifications.' (The Conservatives like to point out that of the 30,000 pupils that got three As in their A-levels last year, only 176 belonged to the 5,000 poorer students eligible for free school meals.)

The workings of educational meritocracy, the erosion of decent working-class jobs, the rise in income inequality and the perceived threats from globalisation/immigration – all these contribute to a widespread disaffection among people towards the bottom of the pile, especially in the big European states. This in turn feeds some of the social problems highlighted by Cameron and Duncan Smith. In some areas, perception does match reality – for example, knife and gun crime and the near-total disregard for authority by youth in poor urban centres. (In 2007-08, 62 per cent of robberies in England and Wales were recorded by just three police forces – the Metropolitan Police, Greater Manchester and West Midlands. Within these regions, crimes were overwhelmingly concentrated among males aged 16-24 in poorer urban areas.)
October 2008

⇨ The above information is an extract from the article *Does Britain need fixing?* and is reprinted with kind permission from Ipsos MORI. To view the full article, visit www.ipsos-mori.com

Violence in street crime

Information from the Economic and Social Research Council

Statistics

⇨ During the research 120 offenders were interviewed. 89 were male and 31 were female.

⇨ The majority were aged 26 plus.

⇨ The majority were white with ten per cent defining themselves as black, 12 per cent as mixed race and one per cent Asian.

⇨ Young men aged between 16 and 24 have the highest risk of being a victim of crime – 13 per cent (British Crime Survey 2007-08).

The character of street crimes is changing. Academics have traditionally seen British street robberies as being carried out by calculating career robbers. More recent research shows that in the 21st century such crimes are 'haphazard, essentially amateur excursions'. Behind this change is an emerging street culture in Britain similar to that in urban United States of America.

Professor Trevor Bennett and his team of researchers at the University of Glamorgan interviewed offenders in prisons and young offenders' institutions. They investigated a variety of violent offences, and looked in particular at the role played by street culture.

Few of the offenders interviewed said they needed money for basic subsistence. Most wanted it to support 'what might be described as a criminal lifestyle', write Wright, Brookman and Bennett in the *British Journal of Criminology* (2006), 'Wherein the pursuit of illicit action generated an ongoing need for "fast cash" that realistically could only be satisfied through crime.'

Some offenders also wanted to be able to show off expensive items, such as cars. 'This was not so much for what the car did but for what it said to others,' the researchers comment.

Sometimes cash itself was the fashion item. One interviewee said: 'I just love money. It's like, I feel big when I got money, like when I haven't got money, it feels like ****.'

Sometimes street robbery is about the excitement of the fight, the fun of

overpowering someone else. 'It wasn't like, for money – I was more addicted to robbing than I was to drugs,' said an offender.

Other reasons for street robbery were revenge and 'debt collecting', for instance if drug dealers are owed money. Offenders often wanted to project themselves as someone not to be messed with. It could also take the form of a rite of passage.

The research concluded that street robbers decide to commit their offences in a social and psychological terrain, containing few realistic alternatives. This is why their behaviour can appear irrational. (They often net little cash and risk long prison sentences.) Desperation, the research showed, led to a mindset in which individuals are too focused on meeting the immediate need – be it to keep the party going, restore personal honour, dissipate anger or exact informal justice – to maximise reward or to think clearly about the possibility of threatened sanctions.

⇨ The above information is reprinted with kind permission from the Economic and Social Research Council. Visit www.esrcsocietytoday.ac.uk for more information on this and other related topics.

© ESRC

The right to fight?

There is nothing new about street fighting as a way to display manliness. In Victorian times, say researchers from Edge Hill University, society tolerated or even condoned such one-on-one violence much more than it does today. However, attitudes began to change by the turn of the century

Dr John Archer and his colleagues who set out to examine working class male-on-male violence and working class notions of masculinity, found there were deeply embedded beliefs about men's right to fight. 'Manly' or 'English' fights, fought between two men according to codes of honour, were dismissed or treated leniently in the courts, even if someone died. However, if a losing fighter drew a knife (not uncommon), the magistrates were tougher. So-called fair fights often degenerated into stabbings.

'Considerable evidence suggests that the notion of the fair fight was in reality, if not quite a fiction, then certainly a contest in which the rules were frequently broken,' say the researchers.

Most male violence was fuelled by alcohol. For unemployed men living in poverty in overcrowded slums, fighting was a way to gain status and self-esteem. Cornermen, as they were known, often fought to assert their

esrc|societytoday

right to stand on a street corner. They went looking for fights in the hope of gaining a reputation for hardness.

In certain parts of town, police ignored street violence. 'Here they left roughs to fight other roughs,' say the researchers.

One contrast with the present day is that those engaging in violent behaviour were somewhat older. Today the most violent group is in their late teens, while in the 1870s-90s more than 75 per cent of men charged with assaulting police were over 20. However, between 1860 and 1900 the age of men prosecuted for common assault got younger.

Newspaper reports showed that from the late 1860s onwards, there was growing criticism of the police for their use of force. In cases which came before the courts, 54 per cent could be described as unprovoked police assaults on the public; 31 per cent arose during arrests and 15 per cent took place in custody. A surprising 40 per cent of the victims were women. The researchers believe that Liverpool police assumed them to be prostitutes, whom they felt able to assault with little fear of prosecution.

Although a child-murder with 'eerie parallels' to the Jamie Bulger case did not provoke a moral panic, the first rail murder (London, July 1864) featured in the press for the following five months. 'The murder of a gentleman in a First Class compartment...suddenly made every rail traveller feel vulnerable to attack.'

⇨ The above information is reprinted with kind permission from the Economic and Social Research Council. Visit www.esrcsocietytoday.ac.uk for more information.

© ESRC

Fear of crime or anxiety about a changing society?

Do we really fear crime or are we just anxious about neighbourhood breakdown and the speed of change in society?

Research, funded by the Economic and Social Research Council, shows that our everyday concerns about crime in England and Wales are much less frequent than previously thought. For people who live in high crime areas, the fear of crime tends to be an everyday experience that reduces their quality of life. Yet for those people who live more protected lives, the fear of crime tends to be a more diffuse feeling that reflects a broader expression of concerns about social change.

Dr Stephen Farrall from Sheffield University and Dr Jonathan Jackson of the London School of Economics found that people did not neatly separate out the issue of crime from general unease towards social stability and the pace and direction of our changing society. Rather than being about an irrational sense of crime,

esrc|societytoday

both fear of crime and anxiety about crime distilled popular concerns about neighbourhood breakdown.

Dr Stephen Farrall said 'the fear of crime is an important social indicator of any society's well-being. Our research suggests however that real, immediate threats to people are, thankfully, rarely encountered.'

Dr Jonathan Jackson added 'fear of crime is more often a broader anxiety than a concrete worry about the threat of victimisation – but in any case,

these emotions are all bound up in public concerns about social change and the health of the norms and values that underpin our society'. *19 May 2008*

Both fear of crime and anxiety about crime distilled popular concerns about neighbourhood breakdown

---

⇨ The above information is reprinted with kind permission from the Economic and Social Research Council. Visit www.esrcsocietytoday. ac.uk for more information.

© ESRC

Concerns about crime and anti-social behaviour

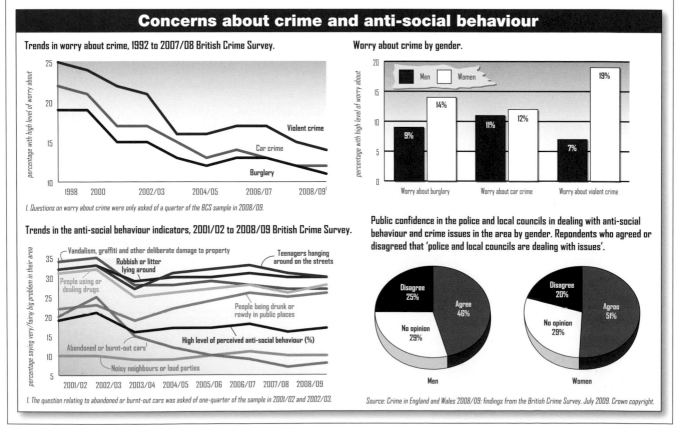

Trends in worry about crime, 1992 to 2007/08 British Crime Survey.

percentage with high level of worry about — Violent crime, Car crime, Burglary (1998, 2000, 2002/03, 2004/05, 2006/07, 2008/09)

1. Questions on worry about crime were only asked of a quarter of the BCS sample in 2008/09.

Worry about crime by gender. (Men / Women)

Worry about burglary: Men 9%, Women 14%
Worry about car crime: Men 11%, Women 12%
Worry about violent crime: Men 7%, Women 19%

Trends in the anti-social behaviour indicators, 2001/02 to 2008/09 British Crime Survey.

percentage saying very/fairly big problem in their area — Vandalism, graffiti and other deliberate damage to property; Rubbish or litter lying around; People using or dealing drugs; Teenagers hanging around on the streets; People being drunk or rowdy in public places; High level of perceived anti-social behaviour (%); Abandoned or burnt-out cars; Noisy neighbours or loud parties (2001/02 – 2008/09)

1. The question relating to abandoned or burnt-out cars was asked of one-quarter of the sample in 2001/02 and 2002/03.

Public confidence in the police and local councils in dealing with anti-social behaviour and crime issues in the area by gender. Repondents who agreed or disagreed that 'police and local councils are dealing with issues'.

Men: Disagree 25%, Agree 46%, No opinion 29%
Women: Disagree 20%, Agree 51%, No opinion 29%

Source: Crime in England and Wales 2008/09: findings from the British Crime Survey. July 2009. Crown copyright.

Weapons and the law

Are you tempted to carry a weapon? Make sure you get the facts before you tool up

An offensive weapon is any object that has been made or adapted to cause injury. This covers anything from purpose-built weapons such as guns and knives, to that snooker cue you've just picked up to swing at somebody.

In defining what counts as a weapon, it means your intention for the object in question could be taken into account. Section 1 of the Prevention of Crime Act 1953 outlaws the possession in any public place of an offensive weapon 'without lawful authority or reasonable excuse'. Laws restricting the sale, carrying, use and production of knives are also contained in the Restriction of Offensive Weapons Act 1959, the Criminal Justice Act 1988, the Criminal Justice and Public Order Act 1994, the Offensive Weapons Act 1996, the Knives Act 1997 and the Violent Crime Reduction Act 2006.

If you're caught with an offensive weapon

In the eyes of the law, it's down to you to show that the weapon in question wasn't made or adapted to cause injury. Claiming that you're carrying a weapon in public for someone else is no excuse. Here's the low-down on the law:

⇨ Should you be arrested, and found guilty of carrying an offensive weapon in public, you could face a fine, imprisonment, or both;

⇨ Carrying a knife could make you liable to a fine of up to £1,000, or a maximum of four years' imprisonment. If it's used to injure or threaten someone the penalties are more severe;

⇨ If you're found guilty of grievous bodily harm you could face life imprisonment;

⇨ If you're found guilty of man-slaughter, attempted murder or murder, your punishment could also be life imprisonment.

Knives in public and in private

It isn't illegal in the UK to own a knife in private (though flick knives, butterfly knives and disguised knives are prohibited). However, if any knife is used in a threatening way in a private environment, it becomes an offensive weapon. It's an offence to carry any knife in public, even if you're not behaving in a threatening manner, and you can face a penalty of two years' imprisonment and a £5,000 fine for doing so.

Legal exceptions for carrying a knife

Under certain circumstances, it's legal to be in possession of a knife in public:

⇨ If it's a tool of the trade (i.e. you work in catering or carpentry);

⇨ For religious reasons (i.e. a Sikh kirpan);

⇨ If it's a penknife (pocket or folding knife) less than three inches long (although it may be considered offensive if carried for the purpose of causing injury or harm).

Handing in a weapon

⇨ Police authorities regularly hold weapons amnesties, in which you're free to hand in an offensive weapon without risk of prosecution;

⇨ Outside of an amnesty your circumstances would dictate how the police would receive you. However, whatever the reason you're in possession of an offensive weapon, police advice is to contact your local station to make arrangements for handing it in;

⇨ If you've simply come across a gun or a flick knife in public, police advice is not to touch it, but report the find by phone or in person at the local station.

Which weapons are illegal?

Knives

It's illegal for anyone under the age of 18 to buy a knife. Flick knives, butterfly knives and disguised knives (hidden in a belt or mobile phone etc) are illegal to everyone. Swiss Army knives are allowed, so long as the blade is under 7.62cm; however, if any knife is used in a threatening way it becomes an offensive weapon. It's an offence to carry a knife in public, and you can face a penalty of two years' imprisonment and a £5,000 fine for doing so. If you're caught with a knife at school you could be sentenced to four years in jail.

Guns

You need to have a licence to own a gun and there are strict restrictions on getting one, such as proving you'll only be using it to kill vermin, or it's an antique-type gun. You also have to get two people to tell the police that you're responsible enough to own a gun.

Airguns

These come under different laws from guns that use bullets. People aged under 18 aren't allowed to buy guns or ammunition. If you are under 18 you can use an airgun at a registered gun club or if someone over the age of 21 is responsible for you. If you're over the age of 17 you can buy guns and ammunition as long as the gun is under the UK legal limit of 12ft.lbs muzzle energy for rifles and 6ft.lbs muzzle energy for pistols. Guns over that limit need a firearms certificate before they can be owned.

⇨ The above information is re-printed with kind permission from TheSite. Visit www.thesite.org for more information.

© TheSite

Anti-social behaviour

Anti-social behaviour includes a range of problems: noisy neighbours, abandoned cars, vandalism, graffiti, litter and intimidating groups. It creates an environment where crime can take hold and affect people's everyday lives. But there are ways to tackle the problem

What you can do

If anti-social behaviour is a problem in your area, you can:

➪ talk to your local anti-social behaviour co-ordinator, who can help you tackle the problem;
➪ get involved to help prevent and tackle anti-social behaviour when it does occur;
➪ report anti-social behaviour incidents;
➪ be a witness to support legal action and stop anti-social behaviour by getting court orders.

In some cases witnesses' identities can be kept anonymous.

Acceptable Behaviour Contract (ABCs)

An ABC is a written agreement made between a person causing anti-social behaviour and their local authority, Youth Inclusion Support Panel, landlord or the police. ABCs are designed to get individuals to acknowledge their anti-social behaviour and the effect it has on others with the aim of stopping that behaviour at an early stage. An ABC sets out the types of anti-social acts the person agrees not to continue and outlines the consequences if the contract is breached.

ABCs, although designed for young people, can be used for offenders of any age. ABCs are informal and flexible so can be used for various types of anti-social behaviour.

ABCs aren't legally binding, but can be referred to in court as evidence in ASBO applications or in eviction or possession proceedings.

Penalty notices

A Fixed Penalty Notice (FPN) and a Penalty Notice for Disorder (PND) are one-off penalties issued to people who commit anti-social behaviour.

Fixed Penalty Notices (FPNs) generally deal with environmental offences like dropping litter, minor graffiti offences, not cleaning up dog fouling or noise nuisance from a private residence during the night. They can be issued by local council officers, police community support officers (PCSOs) and certain other accredited people. They can be issued to anyone over ten years old. Set penalties apply – these are higher for noise-related offences.

Penalty Notices for Disorder (PNDs) are issued for more serious offences, like throwing fireworks or being drunk and disorderly. PNDs can be issued by the police, PCSOs and certain other accredited people.

PNDs can be issued to anyone over 16 years old, the amount of the fine depends on how bad the behaviour is. Examples where a PND may be issued include: behaving in a way likely to cause harassment, alarm or distress to others; being drunk and disorderly in public, selling alcohol to an under 18 year old or breaching a fireworks curfew.

Anti-Social Behaviour Orders (ASBOs)

An ASBO is a court order applied for by local authorities, police forces (including the British Transport Police) and by registered social landlords (these are landlords providing social housing). They cannot be applied for by members of the public, but people do get involved by collecting evidence and helping to monitor breaches.

ASBOs aim to protect the public from further anti-social behaviour from an individual rather than punish the person. They ban the individual from repeating the offending behaviour or entering a set area and last for a minimum of two years.

ASBOs are designed with communities in mind to encourage people to get involved in reporting local crime and anti-social behaviour. They're not criminal penalties so they won't appear on a police record. However, breaching an ASBO is a criminal offence and the punishment for this may be a fine or even imprisonment.

CCTV and anti-social behaviour

CCTV has proved to be a highly effective tool in discouraging anti-social behaviour and providing evidence of crimes.

Powers of dispersal

Groups can be dispersed if they are behaving anti-socially in specific locations. A designated area for dispersal can range in size from a cash point to a whole local authority area, as long as there is evidence of anti-social behaviour.

The local authority must agree and the decision must be published in a local newspaper or by notices in the local area.

Encouraging respect in communities

'Respect' is a campaign to encourage respect in communities, including stamping out anti-social behaviour, by:

➪ supporting or challenging anti-social households;
➪ tackling truancy and anti-social behaviour in schools;
➪ providing activities for younger people;
➪ strengthening local communities;
➪ stronger measures to tackle anti-social behaviour.

➪ The above information is re-printed with kind permission from Directgov. Visit www.direct.gov.uk for more information on this and other related issues.

© Crown copyright

Police 'should break up teen gangs'

Police should be given new powers to break up teenage gangs, says new report

Tough new control orders aimed at breaking up violent teenage gangs are proposed in a new report from the think-tank led by the former Conservative leader Iain Duncan Smith.

The report warns that toughening up anti-gang measures will not be enough to stem the rising tide of gang violence in the UK. Up to 50,000 young people are gang members

The orders – known as Gang Activity Desistance Orders (GADOs) – would be aimed at gang leaders and would be backed by serious penalties – which could include imprisonment.

But the report also warns that toughening up anti-gang measures will not be enough to stem the rising tide of gang violence in the UK. Up to 50,000 young people are gang members.

The report recommends a raft of medium and long-term measures designed to steer teenagers away from the clutches of the street gang.

GADOs would be issued by the courts in areas where serious gang violence is intimidating witnesses and informants and stopping them from helping the police mount prosecutions.

The report is critical of ASBOs, saying that they have been over-used and that their credibility has been undermined by the all-too-frequent failure to punish breaches.

'The Working Group believes that civil orders should be used as a last resort, targeted only at core gang members and used in conjunction with social and education interventions. ASBOs too often do not meet these criteria...

'We recommend that a specialist commission looks into the possibility of creating a gang-specific civil order to tackle high impact players: a Gang Desistance Order (GADO).'

GADOs must be tightly targeted, only used as a last resort and their breach 'must have serious repercussions'.

The report *Dying to Belong* from the think-tank set up by former Conservative leader Iain Duncan Smith recommends that the police actively target gang leaders in line with schemes pioneered by US police and other agencies.

The report also accuses local and national government of a lack of leadership and urgency in tackling the problem.

Drawing on projects that have produced spectacular reductions in gang-related deaths in Boston and other US cities, the Centre for Social Justice (CSJ) study says that ringleaders should be given an ultimatum by police: either stop the violence and we'll ensure you get support or continue and we will do everything in our power to bring you to justice. This would include sustained, daily attention and even minor infractions – such as driving offences – will lead to prosecution.

Areas where gang crime is prevalent should be designated Gang Prevention Zones and made the focus of intensive efforts involving all agencies – including police and local authorities – to reverse gang culture.

The combination of the police pressure and the work of the other agencies in offering a way out for gang members is critical. Support from statutory and non-statutory agencies should include skills training, remedial education, drug rehabilitation and help in finding work.

Mr Duncan Smith said: 'The tragic murder of Rhys Jones in Liverpool has brought home the casual savagery of gang crime in Britain today. Half the 27 teenagers murdered in London last year were the victims of gang crime. That should bring home the brutal truth that street gangs are a nasty and shocking symptom of the broken society.

'We need emergency action in stemming the rise of gang culture which is devastating our most disadvantaged communities. Our report is a practical solution which doesn't just deal with the narrow issue of knives but the vital issue of the people who are most likely to be using knives or any weapon and is founded on the best practice in the Western world.'

The CSJ blueprint for tackling gangs says that there must be a short-, medium- and long-term strategy for turning the tide of criminality. It warns that the number of gangs and their associated crime is rising in Britain's major cities and estimates that 20,000 to 50,000 teenagers are members of violent gangs.

The report runs to 210 pages, has taken 14 months to compile and is based on contacts with over 150 practitioners, police, youth workers and gang members in the UK and Boston and Los Angeles in the USA. It has been drawn up by a 14-strong working group of experts chaired by Simon Antrobus, chief executive of Clubs for Young People.

Mr Antrobus said: 'The critical element of this report is that it goes beyond a traditional approach to responding to the challenge of gangs in our communities. It recognises that gang members are children and young people first – increasingly younger. Similarly it recognises that an approach based on enforcement alone is flawed.

'We need an instant response. But we won't make sustainable progress in reversing this worrying trend that is pulling children and young people on to the street and into the gangs in our inner cities unless we are prepared to engage with the less eye-catching but vital work of medium- and long-term social renewal among our marginalised and disaffected young people.

'The adult world bears a big share of the blame for the rise of the gang, not least because so many of our young men are experiencing a crisis in masculinity. Father deficit and space restriction lead to anger and rage forcing some young men to search for a sense of belonging which they find in the local gang and the gang leader.'

The report says that the immediate challenge is to break up the gangs and redirect their members towards constructive activity. But medium- and long-term measures are also needed to build trust between the police and young people and to prevent a new generation from being lost to gang culture.

The message – that violence will no longer be tolerated – should be communicated through a 'call-in' in which members of different gangs are brought together in a single place, such as a courtroom. The tactic has been successfully used in the United States and in Glasgow.

The report accuses local and national government of failing to take the lead on tackling gangs.

In many areas, the task of tackling gangs has been seen as almost solely the responsibility of the police by politicians - who have made enforcement their main focus and taken an increasingly punitive stance.

It took a community and media outcry for the Government to produce a strategy for tackling gangs as late as May 2008, the report says.

The report says immediate action is needed to disrupt gangs and prevent violence. The Boston Gun Project's Operation Ceasefire had impressive results tackling gangs and violence in the US city – a 63 per cent decrease in youth homicides per month – and this model should inform the UK's response to gangs.

It finds a number of UK initiatives – including Merseyside's Matrix Gun Crime Team and Scotland's Violence Reduction Unit – have implemented the Boston model with very promising early results.

The key elements for a successful gang prevention initiative include:
⇨ A thorough understanding of the local problem and what is driving it;
⇨ Committed and visible leadership at the highest levels;
⇨ Full multi-agency collaboration and communication (data sharing);
⇨ A multi-pronged approach combining enforcement, intervention and prevention;
⇨ An honest and targeted approach;
⇨ Meaningful community engagement.

The report puts forward a definition of a gang – 'a relatively durable, predominantly street-based group of young people who (1) see themselves (and are seen by others) as a discernible group, (2) engage in a range of criminal activity and violence, (3) identify with or lay claim over territory, (4) have some form of identifying structural feature, and (5) are in conflict with other, similar, gangs'. The report is highly critical of the Government for failing to coordinate the use of a standard definition across the country for street gangs, which they believe is one of the reasons why activity has been so confused.

The report finds wide-ranging criminality among gang members from drug dealing and robbery to assault to rape. They are also prolific in their offending. Gang members identified by the Home Office study averaged 11 convictions; separate research found that South Manchester gang members averaged 12 arrests.

Another study found that the six per cent of people self-reporting as gang members were responsible for over a fifth of all core offences and 40 per cent of all burglaries.
11 February 2009

⇨ The above information is reprinted with kind permission from the Centre for Social Justice. Visit www.centreforsocialjustice.org.uk for more information.

Coping with kidulthood

The hidden truth behind Britain's abandoned adolescents

The Transition to Adulthood (T2A) Alliance is a coalition of organisations and individuals working to improve the life chances of young adults between the ages of 18 and 25 who are at risk of falling into the criminal justice system. This report will feed into our work over the coming year and provides the first building block in the creation of a campaign manifesto planned for 2009.

The report is based on two pieces of new empirical research commissioned exclusively for the T2A Alliance:

All the young offenders stated that they had received little if any support from their family, their local community or the education system while growing up

⇨ The first, by the public opinion research company Populus, consists of focus group research comparing the life experiences of a group of male young offenders with a group of male university students.

⇨ The second, by the market research company Com Res, is the result of opinion polling carried out among 1001 young people to test their attitudes towards a broad set of policy initiatives related to youth justice.

Important findings of the focus groups

⇨ All the young offenders stated that they had received little if any support from their family, their local community or the education system while growing up:

'They [students] had parents that were there for them, who provided for them. I've not had that, me. I've had to live off myself.' [Young Offender]

'They [students] have always had MP3 players in their pockets and new trainers, we've had to get it ourselves.' [Young Offender]

'If you stopped a uni student out on the street to get their food tonight, get their bed, and get their clothes for tomorrow they wouldn't know the first f**king thing to do. They'd be pulling out their iPhones and saying "oh, daddy, mummy". They don't know the first thing about how to hustle on the streets.' [Young Offender]

⇨ The young offenders also painted a bleak picture of their local neighbourhood. They spoke of a suffocating environment where crime was prevalent and a climate of fear existed within the community:

'It's a dog-eat-dog world. It's every man for himself.' [Young Offender]

'You all join a firm so that you feel safe. I need my boys. It's a form of survival'. [Young Offender]

'It [gang culture] has always been there, the only thing that's different is the guns have come along. The violence has always been there but there didn't used to be the guns.' [Young Offender]

'It's a survival thing as well, because if people know that you're sick, and people know that if they mess with you then you're going to do something really nasty, then they leave you alone. If they don't think you're likely you're going to get hurt more.' [Young Offender]

'It's different now. Even the kids that you knew years ago – who used to be quiet and never came out – are running around off their head. You're just like "you're not like that, you're not the same kid I knew two years ago but now you're running around chopping people's heads off". The climates changed and everyone thinks that you've got to be like that. You have to prove yourself'. [Young Offender]

⇨ When talking about their day-to-day lives, all the young offenders talked of the twin imperatives of money and respect:

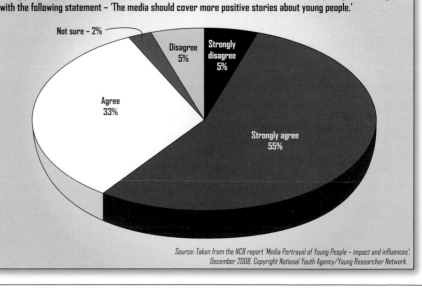

Media portrayal of young people

Young people aged 13-18 surveyed by the NCB were asked: Please indicate to what extent you agree or disagree with the following statement – 'The media should cover more positive stories about young people.'

Not sure – 2%
Disagree 5%
Strongly disagree 5%
Agree 33%
Strongly agree 55%

Source: Taken from the NCB report 'Media Portrayal of Young People – impact and influences'. December 2008. Copyright National Youth Agency/Young Researcher Network.

CRIME   PRISON   PUNISHMENT

'Everything nowadays is about money and reputation. That's why people sell drugs. You sell drugs to make your money, you make your money to make your reputation and just to live.' [Young Offender]

'If you've been out on the graft and you've made the money you're like "it's free money" and you'll spend it on whatever.' [Young Offender]

⇨ Some said that prison – while being a stark punishment – was also a counterproductive environment where they learnt how to commit crime better rather than how to rehabilitate themselves:

'You can go into jail because you've just done something small, but then you're sat there listening to everyone else talking and you're learning new s**t and how to do new things.' [Young Offender]

⇨ Similarly, once released from YOI, they revealed a lack of confidence in the structure put in place to help rehabilitate them into mainstream society through re-housing, work experience or employment:

'If you had a job you probably wouldn't be going out robbing, but then when you go for a job they find you've got a record.' [Young Offender]

Key findings of the polling

⇨ Of the 1001 young people polled 83% say that getting work experience and having good job opportunities is a key factor in helping young people move away from crime.

⇨ 76% also believe that ensuring access to youth clubs and community centres for young people so that they can socialise and interact was important in countering youth crime.

⇨ 82% believe that it is important going to a school that does not tolerate bad behaviour and instils discipline and personal responsibility in its pupils.

⇨ For young people who have drug or alcohol problems 78% think that immediate and regular support by social services is an important way of tackling the problem.

21 December 2008

⇨ The above information is reprinted with kind permission from the Barrow Cadbury Trust. Visit www.bctrust.org.uk for more information on this and other related topics.

© Barrow Cadbury Trust

Gang membership

Top danger signs

Children and Young People's Minister Beverley Hughes is today publishing a consultation on new guidance to help professionals spot the first signs of gang membership.

This guidance is aimed at professionals such as social workers, youth workers and youth offending teams already working with young people displaying risk factors. The guidance highlights risk factors which could signal towards their involvement in gangs. Some high level risk factors are:

⇨ Early problems with anti-social and criminal behaviour;

⇨ Persistent offending;

⇨ Unable to regulate own emotions and behaviour;

⇨ Physical violence and aggression;

⇨ Permanent exclusion from school;

⇨ Friends condoning or involved in anti-social and aggressive behaviour;

⇨ Alcohol and drug misuse.

Anecdotal evidence shows that more children, including girls, are becoming gang members, particularly when they have older siblings involved in gangs. They can quickly become involved in illegal and dangerous activity, putting themselves and others in danger.

When young people do break the law they must be held accountable, but we also need to make sure that youth and social workers are given the help and advice they need to spot the danger signs early and support these children and young people.

The new guidance, developed with the police and local authorities, lists 16 signs that should ring alarm

bells and will be sent to thousands of youth and social workers later this year. It outlines what signs to look for, what traits make a young person most 'at-risk' of getting caught up in a gang and provides an overview of support and intervention that are available to anyone working with young people.

'Early intervention is key in preventing young people from falling into the cycle of violence and crime linked to street gangs'

Minister for Children and Young People Beverley Hughes said:

'Involvement in gang activity is a very real and complex issue facing many children and young people, and this guidance aims to help early detection, intervention and support for those most at risk.

'People working with young people at risk are ideally placed to spot the early signs of gang involvement and we want them to be aware of these top danger signs to make sure identifying them becomes a routine but essential part of their work.

'Lots of work is already being done by those who work with young people and across Government to tackle the problem of gangs, both from a wider preventative perspective and a public protection angle. And when younger brothers and sisters are in danger of being drawn into gangs it's a child safety issue too and every means of protecting them must be used, including holding parents to account. Working together is the only way we can intervene early and help young people stay away from the harm caused by gang activity.'

Some tell-tale signs that young people, who already display high risk factors, might be involved in gangs include:

⇨ holds unexplained money or possessions;
⇨ dropped out of positive activities;
⇨ new nickname;
⇨ graffiti-style 'tags' on possessions, school books, walls;
⇨ constantly talking about another young person who seems to have a lot of influence over them;
⇨ expressing aggressive or intimidating views towards other groups of young people, some of whom may have been friends in the past;
⇨ concerned by the presence of unknown youths in their neighbourhoods.

Home Secretary Jacqui Smith said:

'Early intervention is key in preventing young people from falling into the cycle of violence and crime linked to street gangs. Last year we published *Gangs: You and Your Child*, a guide aimed at helping parents, carers and guardians to spot the early signs of a young person's possible involvement in gangs. It also offered practical advice on the steps they can take if they suspect their child is already in a gang and who to contact for help and support. The new guide being launched today offers further practical advice to professionals who work with young people to help them spot the danger signs and act.

'We recently widened the focus of the Tackling Knives Action Programme to include serious youth violence and gangs. Maintaining this targeted approach is part of wider government action to continue clamping down on the small minority of young people who commit violent crime.'

18 March 2009

⇨ The above information is reprinted with kind permission from the Department for Children, Schools and Families. Visit www.dcsf.gov.uk for more information.

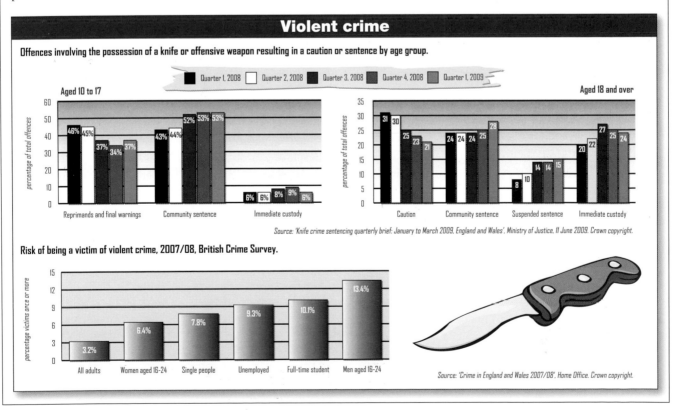

Violent crime

Offences involving the possession of a knife or offensive weapon resulting in a caution or sentence by age group.

Quarter 1, 2008 | Quarter 2, 2008 | Quarter 3, 2008 | Quarter 4, 2008 | Quarter 1, 2009

Aged 10 to 17

percentage of total offences

Reprimands and final warnings: 46%, 45%, 37%, 34%, 37%
Community sentence: 43%, 44%, 52%, 53%, 53%
Immediate custody: 6%, 6%, 8%, 9%, 6%

Aged 18 and over

percentage of total offences

Caution: 31, 30, 25, 23, 21
Community sentence: 24, 24, 24, 25
Suspended sentence: 8, 10, 14, 14, 15
Immediate custody: 20, 22, 27, 25, 24

Source: 'Knife crime sentencing quarterly brief: January to March 2009, England and Wales', Ministry of Justice, 11 June 2009. Crown copyright.

Risk of being a victim of violent crime, 2007/08, British Crime Survey.

percentage victims once or more

All adults: 3.2%
Women aged 16-24: 6.4%
Single people: 7.8%
Unemployed: 9.3%
Full-time student: 10.1%
Men aged 16-24: 13.4%

Source: 'Crime in England and Wales 2007/08', Home Office. Crown copyright.

Get rid of 'gangs'

A new report from the Runnymede Trust[i] has found that attempts to label youth violence as a 'gang problem' may be stopping the police and youth services from taking effective preventative action and risks criminalising all young people – especially young black men

The tragic and disturbing patterns of violence between young people are a legitimate cause for concern but the attribution of this tragic violence to 'gangs' obscures more than it illuminates and is stopping effective action being taken to tackle the violence. There is no agreement on the definition of a gang or any intelligence on the number of gangs in our towns and cities. Instead there is speculation, myth-making and confusion. This is not a basis on which to take the necessary action to make our streets safer – especially when they are policies that target young people from minority communities for police action.

> **'With a growing divide between generations and high levels of fear of crime, we do not need mythical "gangs" added to the equation'**

The report[ii], written by Dr Claire Alexander, author of *The Asian Gang*[iii] and a trustee of Runnymede, examines police intelligence gathering, media reporting and the latest academic research. It concludes that:

⇨ While the 'gang' label may be appropriate in a few very specific cases, given the difficulty in agreeing definition and usage, it would be better to abandon this term completely. Certainly 'the gang' should not provide a basis for welfare intervention, legal categorisation or punitive sentencing.

⇨ While the 'gang' might make sense in an American context, interventions on the streets of LA are not transferable to the streets of the UK.

RUNNYMEDE

⇨ There does not seem to be any boundary between young people socialising together in public spaces and 'gang' activity – causing groups of young people to be viewed as automatically suspicious. 'Gangs' are regularly identified as 'cultural' and then attached to particular ethnic groups. The effect is that entire 'communities' are criminalised on the basis of their 'cultures'.

⇨ Intervention into youth conflict needs to be made on the basis of empirically grounded evidence, local understanding and expertise.

⇨ Youth initiatives should avoid the labelling and criminalisation of young people as 'gang members', and resist the linking of state-funded youth initiatives to a 'gang prevention' agenda. Youth initiatives must respond to the real needs of young people in our communities, not just those who fit the image of 'the gangster'.

Rob Berkeley, Deputy Director of Runnymede, said:

'With a growing divide between generations and high levels of fear of crime, we do not need mythical "gangs" added to the equation. More worryingly, talk about use of indiscriminate stop and search will worsen community relations and only serve to distract police from intelligence-led policing into harassing young men because of their supposed gang membership. We deserve better.'

Notes

i The Runnymede Trust is an independent policy research organisation focusing on equality and justice through the promotion of a successful multi-ethnic society. Founded as a Charitable Education Trust, Runnymede has a long track record in policy research, working in collaboration with eminent thinkers and policymakers in the public, private and voluntary sectors. Since 1968, the date of Runnymede's foundation, we have worked to establish and maintain a positive image of what it means to live affirmatively within a society that is both multi-ethnic and culturally diverse. Runnymede continues to speak with a thoughtful and independent public voice on these issues today. For further information visit www.runnymedetrust.org

ii *(Re)thinking Gangs* is released on Monday 16 June 2008 by the Runnymede Trust. It is available for download from www.runnymedetrust.org

iii Dr Claire Alexander is Reader in Sociology at the London School of Economics. Her research interests are in the area of race, ethnicity, masculinity and youth identities, particularly in relation to ethnography. Her main publications include *The Art of Being Black* (OUP, 1996) and *The Asian Gang* (Berg, 2000). She is co-editor of *Beyond Difference* (*Ethnic and Racial Studies*, July 2002) and *Making Race Matter: Bodies, Space and Identity* (Palgrave, 2005) and editor of *Writing Race: Ethnography and Difference* (*Ethnic and Racial Studies*, May 2006). Dr Alexander is a Trustee of the Runnymede Trust.

16 June 2008

⇨ The above information is reprinted with kind permission from the Runnymede Trust. Visit www.runnymedetrust.org for more.

© *Runnymede Trust*

Gun and knife crime survey

Information from 11 MILLION

A survey of more than 1,700 children and young people by 11 MILLION and YouGov today reveals the level of concern children and young people have over gun and knife crime.

More than one in six of those aged eight to 17 say they believe knife crime is a problem in their area – and this more than doubles to 36 per cent of young people from London.

Seven per cent say gun crime is an issue where they live – and this rises to 18 per cent of young people from lower socio-economic groups in Manchester.

But the anonymous poll also shows that only two per cent of those aged 12 to 17 actually carry a knife illegally, with fear or self-protection the most common reason given. And, of those 968 12 to 17 year olds questioned, only four respondents said they had been in possession of a gun illegally.

Young people also make a clear distinction between what they think the responses should be for possession of a knife and possession of a gun, or use of a knife or gun.

For a young person caught carrying a knife, young people favoured non-custodial options, such as education about the risks, dangers and consequences, or curfews. But custody was seen as the best deterrent for those caught carrying a gun, and young people also wanted longer custodial sentences to deal with serious gun or knife offences.

Sir Al Aynsley-Green, the Children's Commissioner for England, who leads the 11 MILLION organisation, said: 'There have been a number of fatal stabbings or shootings of teenagers in the last couple of years – every one has been tragic and they rightly attract attention.

'But at the same time, it is vital that we do not breed fear among young people – we know fear and self-protection are the main reasons why young people carry knives and we must try to reduce that.

'That means all adults, from politicians, to police, to media, taking a responsible line on this, and reassuring young people, rather than frightening or accusing them.'

Sir Al, who tomorrow will publish research analysing the effectiveness of interventions used by agencies to tackle gun and knife crime, added: 'That young people favour non-custodial options for possession of a knife, but not for other gun and knife offences, underlines the fact that fear is so often why some young people carry a knife.

'Sentencing responses to knife possession must address the knife carrying so it is not repeated.'

In terms of relations with the police, more than 80 per cent of children and young people aged 8 to 17 say they like the police – but less than half believe the police respect them.

More than one in six of those aged 8 to 17 say they believe knife crime is a problem in their area – and this more than doubles to 36 per cent of young people from London

---

The poll also reveals that the police are seen as good role models by a quarter of children and young people and are trusted to give good advice about gun and knife crime, while joining the police is one of the top career choices.

Many also feel safer rather than under threat when they see police officers in their area.

But the percentage of young people who like the police decreases with age – 70 per cent of those aged 16 and 17 like the police, down from 90 per cent of those aged eight, nine, ten and eleven.

They also trust the police less the older they get, see others as better role models and think the police respect them less than younger children.

On stop and search, there is some support among young people for more to be carried out to reduce gun and knife crime, and for more police to be on the streets to keep them safe.

But of those who had been stopped and searched, 39 per cent thought less

of the police afterwards – while only nine per cent had a better view.

Sir Al said improving relations between the police and teenagers was vital if gun and knife crime was to be tackled.

'It's commonly thought that young people don't like the police – but this survey shows that, although good relations cool as young people get older, they do actually like the police, trust them and see them as good role models,' Sir Al added.

'But there is clear daylight between what they think of the police and what they believe the police think of them. The stop and search statistics suggest that young people are not against the tactic – but that they want it carried out with respect.

'The police – through the likes of the Association of Chief Police Officers (ACPO) and the Tackling Knives Action Programme (TKAP) – are working hard on improving engagement with young people, with police youth forums, training and Safer Schools officers all contributing to better relations.

'It is vital this continues so that relations continue to improve, and

so that all young people can look to the police for the reassurance they do offer, rather than believe that they need weapons to protect themselves.'

A 16 year old from Merseyside, who has been working on 11 MILLION's gun and knife crime project, said: 'I don't mind being stopped and searched, it's just the way the police do it. At the moment they just seem to stop and search you if you're in a group with your mates or if you're wearing a hood. But you're not doing anything wrong. It would be much better if young people and the police got on better because then there would be more trust and we could maybe help each other.'

Deputy Assistant Commissioner Alfred Hitchcock, who heads TKAP for ACPO, said: 'ACPO strongly supports this comprehensive survey carried out by 11 MILLION, which really gets to the heart of young people's views.

'The numbers of young people who commit or suffer serious violent crime are, thankfully, a small proportion of the total. While most young people go about their lives and are law-abiding citizens, there is still a small percentage

of young people, around two per cent, who admit to carrying knives and go on to commit offences.'

The 11 MILLION/YouGov poll saw more than 1,718 young people aged 8 to 17 surveyed online between 5 December and 15 December 2008.

The survey is listed under Publications on the 11 MILLION website (www.11million.org.uk).

This number was made up of 1,032 children and young people aged 8 to 17, nationally (England) representative of age and gender, and an additional 686 children and young people aged 8 to 17 from C2DE families and living in seven urban areas (London, Liverpool, Manchester, Birmingham, Nottingham, Essex and Leeds) whose police forces are part of the TKAP. Data have been weighted to be representative of 8 to 17 year olds in England.
15 March 2009

⇨ The above information is taken from an 11 MILLION/YouGov survey and is reprinted with permission. Visit www.11million.org.uk for more information.

© 11 MILLION

Youth justice

Information from the Prisoners' Families Helpline

What age range do youth courts deal with?

Youth courts deal with charges against young people aged 10-17. Those aged 10-13 are classified as 'children', 14-17 year olds as 'young persons'. Children under the age of 10 are deemed by law to be incapable of being guilty of a crime. Civil care or supervision proceedings such as child safety or child curfew orders or making the child a ward of court may be used for this age group.

Are young people ever tried in adult courts?

Youth courts will deal with all charges against young people, unless:
⇨ they are charged with a serious crime that, if they were adults, carries a sentence of more than 14 years.

These cases go to the Crown court;
⇨ they are jointly charged with a person aged 18 or over. These cases go to the adult courts.

How do youth courts differ from adult courts?

Youth court proceedings take place in a separate area from the adult court. The magistrates will have undergone special training to sit in youth courts, where procedures are slightly more informal than in adult criminal courts. In order to engage with young defendants, magistrates deliberately talk directly to them rather than through their legal representative. Sentences are meant to specifically address the needs of young offenders. Young defendants should be accompanied by a 'responsible

adult' (this means someone who has care and control of the young person, for example a parent, guardian or carer) when they appear in court unless they are mature enough to be considered independent. All young people appearing in court are entitled to be represented by a solicitor. Access to the youth courts is restricted. This means that there is no public gallery and in most cases there are restrictions on press reporting; for example, no identifying details or pictures of defendants or young witnesses. However, the magistrates can apply to the Director of Public Prosecutions to dispense with the restrictions in exceptional circumstances. Crime victims can attend hearings, but they must make a request to the court if they wish to do so.

What if a young person reaches 18 during a case?

Once the youth court has agreed to hear the case, they retain jurisdiction unless circumstances change. It may, however, refer to an adult court for sentence after a finding of guilt.

What sentences do youth courts give?

⇨ Discharge: absolute – given when the young person admits guilt or is found guilty, but no penalty is imposed, or conditional – no penalty provided that the young person commits no further offence within a specified period. A conditional discharge is now rarely given by the courts.

⇨ Fine: should reflect the seriousness of the offence and the ability of the young person, or of their parent/guardian (if the young person is under 16), to pay. Maximum £250 for child and £1,000 for young person.

⇨ Compensation order: requiring the young person or their parent/guardian to pay compensation (up to £5,000) for any injury (physical or mental, and including terror or distress), loss or damage caused. Takes priority over any costs or fine. Available for all ages, but for youths aged 10-15 it is the parent/guardian who has to pay, unless it is unreasonable or they cannot be found. For 16-17 year olds, the parent/guardian may be ordered to pay.

⇨ Referral order: can be given to a young person who pleads guilty to an offence when it is her/his first time in court. Requires the young person to agree a contract of behaviour with their parents/guardians and the victim (where appropriate), addressing the harm caused by the offence and the causes of the offending behaviour. The contract lasts between 3 and 12 months. The conviction is 'spent' once the contract has been successfully completed. This means that in most circumstances the offence will not have to be disclosed when applying for work.

⇨ Attendance centre order: requires attendance at specified centre.

Can last up to 36 hours. The main purpose of attendance centres is to put a restriction on young offenders' leisure time and for such time to be used more constructively. Attendance centres are open on Saturdays for two or three hours. Their programmes concentrate on group work to give attendees basic skills – for example literacy and numeracy, life skills, cookery, first aid, money management, as well as sessions aimed at raising awareness of victim, drug, alcohol-related and sexual health matters.

Youth courts deal with charges against young people aged 10-17. Children under the age of 10 are deemed by law to be incapable of being guilty of a crime

---

⇨ Reparation order: designed to help young offenders understand the consequences of their behaviour. They require the young person to repair the harm caused by their offence either directly to the victim (this can involve victim/offender mediation if both parties agree) or indirectly to the community. Examples include cleaning up graffiti or undertaking community work. Programmes of work are developed by Youth Offending Teams (YOTs). Last for a maximum of 24 hours over a period of three months.

⇨ Action plan order: three-month, intensively supervised community service programme focusing on education and involving the young person's parents/guardians. Aimed at addressing the cause of offending. It can include repairing the harm done to the victim or the community or attending an Attendance Centre. Supervised by the YOT.

⇨ Supervision order: lasting up to three years. A range of conditions can be attached to the order when

the sentence is used for more serious offences. These are called 'specified activities' and can last for up to 90 days. Examples include curfews or being required to live at a specified address, which could be a probation hostel; to attend a probation centre or other activity; or to undergo treatment.

⇨ Community rehabilitation order: for 16/17 year olds only. Equivalent to a supervision order, but for this specific age range. Supervised by a YOT and can include activities such as repairing the harm caused by their offence and programmes to address offending behaviour, like anger management. Minimum six months – maximum three years.

⇨ Community punishment order: 16/17 year olds only. Unpaid work in the community supervised by probation officer. 40 hours to 240 hours, within 12 months. Work can include carpentry, conservation, working with the elderly.

⇨ Community punishment and rehabilitation order: 16/17 year olds only. Elements of community and community punishment orders. At least 12 months probation and 40-100 hours service.

⇨ Curfew order: requires to remain in a specified place for set periods of time, which can be between 2-12 hours a day, for up to six months.

⇨ Detention and training order: For 12-17 year olds. Sentences a young person to custody. Only given by the courts to young people who represent a high level of risk, have a significant offending history or are persistent offenders and where no other sentence will manage their risks effectively. The seriousness of the offence is always taken into account. The length of the sentence can be between four months and two years. The first half of the sentence is spent in custody while the second half is spent in the community under the supervision of the YOT. The court can require the young person to be on an Intensive Supervision and Surveillance Programme (ISSP) as a condition of the community period of the sentence. The court takes time spent on remand into account before passing sentence.

⇨ Drug treatment and testing order: for those aged 16 and over who are dependent on drugs and likely to benefit from treatment. Lasts between six months and three years. The young person consents to an order requiring that they undergo drug treatment and regular testing by a drug treatment provider and is supervised by the probation services. Reviews take place monthly, following which changes can be made to the order.

⇨ Binding over: a young person or her/his parent/guardian can be bound over to be of good behaviour, i.e. to promise not to offend on pain of forfeiting a sum of money fixed by the court.

⇨ Anti-Social Behaviour Order (ASBO): a civil order which can incur criminal sanctions if breached. Can be used against anyone who is ten years of age or over and has behaved in a manner that caused or was likely to cause harassment, alarm or distress to someone not living in the household. An ASBO stops the young person from going to particular places or doing particular things. The minimum duration is two years and the maximum period is five years. 10-17 year olds can have an individual support order (ISO) attached to their ASBO, which imposes positive conditions aimed at addressing the underlying causes of the offending behaviour. An ISO lasts up to six months and can require a young person to attend up to two sessions a week under the supervision of the YOT. Breach of an ISO is a criminal offence and can be punished by a financial penalty.

⇨ Child Safety Order: only for children under 10 who have committed an offence, breached a local Child Curfew or caused harassment, distress or alarm. A social worker or officer from the YOT supervises the child. If the order is not complied with, the parent can be made the subject of a

parenting order. Parenting orders can require parents/carers to attend counselling and guidance sessions where they receive help in dealing with their children if they have offended, been truant or have received a Child Safety Order, Anti-Social Behaviour Order or Sexual Offences Prevention Order. Sessions last up to three months. Parents may also have other conditions imposed on them such as attending meetings with teachers or ensuring their child does not visit a particular place unsupervised or ensuring their child is at home at particular times. These conditions can last for a period up to 12 months. Parenting orders do not result in the parent/carer getting a criminal record but failure to keep to the terms of an order can lead to prosecution.

⇨ Sex Offenders Notification: requirement to notify the police when found guilty of certain sexual offences. The offender must attend a specified police station within three days of the order being made (or within three days of release if sentenced to custody). The offender must inform the police of their name, date of birth, home address and national insurance number. They must also notify the police of any change of name or address, if they are away from home for a period of seven days or more in any 12-month period, or if they intend to leave the UK. The length of the registration period differs according to the sentence received: custodial sentence of more than six months – five years; custodial sentence of six months or less, or in cases of detention in hospital under mental health legislation – three and a half years; any other sentence – two and a half years.

⇨ Sexual Offences Prevention Order: can only be made following an application by the Chief Officer of Police in respect of a convicted sex offender or on finding of guilt for a relevant offence. The court must be satisfied that an order is necessary to protect the public, or any particular members of the

public, from serious sexual harm from the defendant. The effect of the order is to protect the public from the risks posed by placing restrictions on the defendant's behaviour. It is for the court to decide what prohibitions are reasonable in light of the evidence. Minimum duration is five years; there is no upper limit.

⇨ Deferred sentence: available for all youths. Sentencing can be postponed for up to six months but the court must be satisfied it is in the interests of justice to do so. Conditions may be attached to the terms of a deferred sentence. The offender should be set targets they can achieve during the period of deferment. If the defendant complies, they can expect a lower sentence than would otherwise be imposed. Used sparingly.

⇨ The above information is an extract from information provided by the Prisoners' Families Helpline and is reprinted with permission. Visit www.prisonersfamilieshelpline.org. uk for more information or to view the full article.

© Prisoners' Families Helpline

Too young to be a criminal

In the UK, our age of criminal responsibility is set too low, rendering it meaningless and inhumane

What do Turkey, Korea, Morocco, Uganda, Algeria, Uzbekistan, China, the Russian Federation and Egypt have in common? One is that they all have political regimes that most British people would find it intolerable to live under. Another is that these countries all set their age of criminal responsibility at a level higher than England and Wales (currently age ten) and Scotland (eight).

The lower age of criminal responsibility 'shall not be fixed at too low an age level, bearing in mind the facts of emotional, mental and intellectual maturity'

Looked at another way, at what age should a child be able to decide to get a tattoo on their arm? Some might feel that the current legal age of 18 is too high. Few would argue that primary school children should be able to decide for themselves. Or what of the legal right to vote, currently set at 18? There is an ongoing debate about whether it should be lowered to 16. But would anyone seriously propose it should be lowered to 12, or possibly ten?

A young person cannot get married until they are 18, or 16 with the consent of their parents. As for sex, a young person has to be 16 before they can be said to have consented to sex. Anyone suggesting that a 10- or 12-year-old child might freely consent to sex would attract disapproving glances and disbelief. In some circumstances they might be reported to the police.

There are good reasons why Britain and other countries set minimum ages at which children and young people are allowed to make decisions without appropriate adult oversight and consent. It is related to judgments about a child's intellectual, emotional and mental maturity. No child should be placed in a position where they are making far-reaching decisions about their future without appropriate adult support, guidance and, in some circumstances, veto. Adults take responsibility for decisions affecting children and young people because the children do not necessarily have the capacity to do so themselves.

According to the United Nations, the same principles should apply to the age of criminal responsibility. The Beijing Rules for the administration of juvenile justice, adopted by the General Assembly in 1985, specifies that the lower age of criminal responsibility 'shall not be fixed at too low an age level, bearing in mind the facts of emotional, mental and intellectual maturity'. It goes on to argue that countries should 'consider whether a child can live up to the moral and psychological components of criminal responsibility' and notes that if the age of criminal responsibility is set too low 'the notion of responsibility would become meaningless'. On this basis the minimum age of criminal responsibility in the UK should be 16. Probably it should be 18.

In the UK, our notions about criminal responsibility are meaningless. We set the age of criminal responsibility too low because adult society does not have the collective capacity to imagine a system for dealing humanely with children and young people who break laws created by adults, largely to police the behaviour of adults. We prefer to punish children and young people, so relieving ourselves of the responsibility of thinking seriously about what it would mean to treat children and young people with compassion, dignity and respect.

5 February 2009

© Guardian News & Media Ltd 2009

Be warned: I'm keeping an eye on you!

Young people, crime and public perceptions

Information from the Local Government Education and Children's Services Research Programme

Introduction

Offending amongst young people has been at the centre of public and policy makers' attention in recent years. Media coverage of high-profile cases and the frequent portrayal of hooded teenagers terrorising communities would suggest that young people are becoming increasingly criminalised. The image of young people today appears to be under threat and public perceptions matter – especially as government agendas and policies are shaped by the concerns and attitudes of society. This review of literature on youth crime and public opinion attempts to establish the facts by asking the following questions:

⇨ Has there been a change in the levels of youth crime in recent years?

⇨ What is the current public perception of youth crime? Does the public's perception of youth crime correspond with actual levels of offending amongst young people?

⇨ Where perceptions of crime differ greatly from the reality, what are the underlying reasons for this?

Overall crime levels

Evidence from different sources indicates that overall crime levels have recently stabilised after a period of decline. Self-report surveys such as the British Crime Survey (BCS) reveal that the number of crimes increased through the 1980s and early 1990s, peaking in 1995. The levels of crime then decreased and have been stable since 2005/06 (Jansson, 2007). In addition, comparing 2005/06 with 2006/07, the BCS shows no significant change in crime for the second year running (Nicholas et al., 2007). These trends are echoed in the official crime statistics, which cover offences recorded by the police.

Trends in youth crime

Within this context there are, however, difficulties in presenting an accurate picture of youth offending due to data-collection and recording issues, such as the absence of long-term, self-report studies and changes to legislation that can affect the numbers of young people entering the criminal justice system. 'Detected' youth crime shows signs of some increase in recent years (after a period of long-term decline) but this may be associated with factors unrelated to the actual crime levels, such as a political focus on antisocial behaviour and breaches of subsequent orders. In contrast, self-report studies do not indicate a rise in overall offending levels amongst young people. The evidence appears contradictory and it is easy, therefore, to see how statistics can be used to give an entirely false impression of crime levels – especially when viewed and interpreted in isolation from their broader contexts.

Public perceptions of youth crime

The literature has shown that the public's view of youth crime is a relatively under-researched area, with little systematic attempt to define and measure public opinion. From the few studies completed, it can be said that there is a tendency for the public to overestimate the scale of youth crime, the numbers of young offenders, the proportion of overall crimes committed by young people, and the seriousness (especially in terms of violence) of youth crime. The literature suggests that perceptions of youth crime are not always based on personal experiences and it has been suggested that 'perceptions of prevalence tend to outstrip direct experience of youth crime' (Anderson et al., 2005). This phenomenon also implies that external factors (such as media reporting) have a role to play in shaping the public's view of youth crime.

The National Foundation for Educational Research (NFER) conducted a separate piece of statistical analysis using public perception data from the Best Value User Survey 2006/07 and Youth Justice Board annual offending data 2005/06. No correlation was found between the two sets of data, which again suggests that there is no relationship between perceptions of youth behaviour and the actual prevalence of youth offences. For example, one would expect more negative perceptions in high-crime areas, compared to areas where recorded offences are low. As no relationship was apparent, other factors rather than direct experience of 'youth crime' may be responsible for contributing to a mismatch between the perceptions and reality of such behaviour.

Reasons for public perceptions

The literature identified a range of factors that may influence and shape public opinion and perceptions of crime levels, although much of this content does not have a specific focus on youth crime.

⇨ Media and information – media coverage has a role to play in the mismatch between the perception and reality of youth crime through, for example, the selective reporting of the most serious and high-profile offences.

⇨ Personal characteristics and circumstances – these may impact on the way in which certain people in certain contexts view 'youth crime'. Age, gender, location and socio-economic contexts may have a significant role to play.

⇨ Approaches to youth and 'youth crime' – the way in which youth crime is approached by legislature and criminal justice agencies can impact on public perceptions. Certain behaviour and activities that may, in the past, have been considered to be less serious in nature may now be associated with criminality. A key development here is seen to have been the introduction of Anti-Social Behaviour Orders (ASBOs). It is suggested that ASBOs have an element of predisposition, whereby a breach of an order will automatically criminalise an individual, potentially supporting public perceptions and fears of increasing levels of juvenile crime.

Conclusions and recommendations

Long-term, self-report offending surveys for measuring youth crime

It is generally acknowledged that official crime statistics are subject to many inherent limitations, e.g. changes to police recording practices and the absence of crimes unreported by the public. Therefore, in order to shed light on the realities of youth crime, alternative sources of information on youth offending behaviour are essential. Although self-report studies have been conducted, they have been done intermittently and therefore it is difficult to make confident assertions about long-term trends in youth crime. The absence of corroboratory evidence on youth crime means that it would be hard to evaluate the true impact of strategies or policies that seek to address youth offending.

A long-term, self-report offending survey for young people along the lines of the BCS would make a valuable addition to this analysis of criminal behaviour.

Better definition and measurement of public attitudes

An analysis of public perceptions of youth crime would benefit from more precise definition and measurement. For example, the research shows that the public wrongly attributes a large proportion of offending to young people or believes that youth offending has rapidly escalated – is this simply a case of being misinformed or is the public genuinely concerned and fearful of youth crime? It may be that better dissemination of crime data is required

so that the public is given accurate and understandable information.

A balanced representation of young people

In recent years, national priorities and local services have sought to tackle problems such as anti-social behaviour and youth offending. However, raising the public's awareness of these issues can convey a negative impression of young people as a whole. While such problems rightly deserve attention, there is the danger that young people can become labelled and 'demonised'. In order to avoid fuelling this negativity, local authorities perhaps need to evaluate their communication strategies and consider how they might affect the profile of young people in the area. For example, publicising steps to tackle anti-social behaviour may offer reassurance to some, but highlighting the problem in this way could stimulate fear or concern in others. Thus, local authorities need to achieve a balance between responding to youth crime concerns and profiling the positive activities of young people in the area.

Evidence from different sources indicates that overall crime levels have recently stabilised after a period of decline

---

Building bridges in the community

The attitudes and perceptions of community members lacking direct positive contact with young people, may be disproportionately shaped by external sources of information such as tabloid newspapers and TV reporting. The possible bias conveyed via such media may need to be addressed in order to counteract these negative messages. It may be beneficial to focus on strategies to bring together communities, so that perceptions and opinions are informed more by direct personal experiences rather than exaggerated media representations. The need to build community cohesion has been recognised in *Aiming High*, the Government's ten-year strategy for positive activities:

The level of fear and mistrust at play

today undermines community cohesion and corrodes the stake young people need to feel they have in society.

HM Treasury and DCSF, 2007

It goes on to advocate the creation of positive activities, such as volunteering and intergenerational activities, to build better relations across the generations.

Identifying and responding to public concern

Given that there is variation in how different members of the community view crime, it would be worth pinpointing those groups where concern is most prevalent. In this way, strategies to address public anxiety could be most effectively targeted. For example, public information campaigns regarding local authority plans to tackle anti-social behaviour could focus on particular localities, thereby reassuring residents that something is being done. Equally, community work to foster better relations could be directed towards residents who are likely to be most fearful of youth crime.

Final comment

The problem of youth crime is not simply related to an objective number of criminal actions. The 'problem' also depends on how we, as individuals and as a society, feel about it and how we deal with it. Dealing with the problem will require a two-pronged approach. On one level, there is the need to reduce the incidence of youth crime and to divert young people away from criminal activity. On another level, the public's concern about youth crime requires attention and, as we have found, the degree of concern can be unrelated to the scale of crime. Clearly, there is some work to be done on responding to public concern and making sure there is accurate information about both the levels of youth crime/anti-social behaviour, as well as strategies to tackle the problem where it exists.

May 2008

⇨ Halsey, K. and White, R. (2008). *Young People, Crime and Public Perceptions: a Review of the Literature* (LGA Research Report F/SR264). Slough: NFER.

© Local Government Association/NFER

The fear of young people damages us all

If we demonise an entire generation, we'll pay the price, says Tanya Byron

You may not know the word, but you've probably had the feeling. 'Ephebiphobia', or 'fear of youth', is one of the most enduring phenomena in our society – and it's more prevalent than ever.

An ephebiphobic society is one that views young people in negative and judgmental terms, where the media report (with barely disguised glee) the latest hideous crimes and abuses of our young, which invents devices such as the Mosquito (which emits a high-frequency sound painful to the young) to move pestilent youths along. So worried are we by stories of bad behaviour that we become hyper-protective towards our own children, raising them almost in captivity, cooped up indoors, while letting them do their socialising and risk-taking in the unregulated spaces of the Internet.

But this fear and suspicion are counterproductive. If you tell someone they are a failure enough times, they will be. If you blacken the reputations of the many by the actions of the few, you discriminate. If you design a herd-mentality education system, built around targets and testing, you lose those that require individualised support.

The voices in the debate are loud and numerous, and often remind me of the way in which we used to address racial or sexual imbalance. To comment that 'I see young people behaving like hooligans all the time' implies that what is seen is representative of the general state of things, and that enables discrimination to flourish.

Yes, there are some hideously behaved young people, aggressive and violent. There are gangs and groups that wander aimlessly, drinking, smoking and behaving in an anti-social fashion. There are classrooms where staff are terrorised. These young people exist, and their behaviour has to be dealt with. But if you suggest that they are vulnerable and need understanding and support, you are labelled a wet liberal.

After many years working with some of the most aggressive and destructive children in the country, my views are as clear as the evidence. We fear young people. We stigmatise young people. We discriminate against young people.

Children need boundaries and authority. They need manners and respect for others. They need sanctions and consequences to help them learn. But they will only respect if they are respected, will only learn if their strengths and needs are individually understood, and will only strive if they feel valued and encouraged.

Today's young people face a stream of stories about their peer group that only emphasise the most damaged and disturbed. These skew the perceptions of our society. At Edge Hill University, where I am Chancellor, we have programmes that let 500 learners a year, of all ages, who do not have A-levels, realise their potential without incurring any financial cost. Selection is based on individuals' potential and motivation, with the aim of opening doors to careers ordinarily shut to them.

Yet some see this as 'dumbing down'. I wish the sceptics would come and visit an institution that challenges educational elitism and lets those who have struggled engage their academic abilities. I'd take them round myself. Because while we blame, label and misunderstand an entire generation, because of the actions of a minority of their peers, we can only devalue and never empower.

This isn't about making excuses. It's about challenging a society that discriminates against its youth, and so excludes them from shaping the cultural and social landscape and embracing their futures. In other words, we are an ephebiphobic society – and we should be ashamed of ourselves.

17 March 2009
© *Telegraph Media Group Limited (2009)*

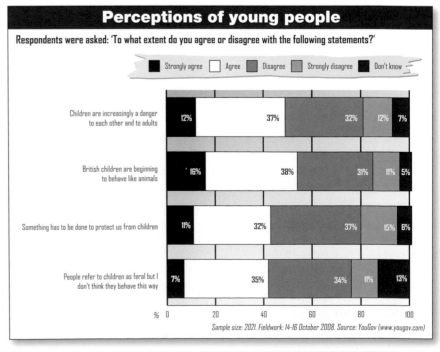

Perceptions of young people

Respondents were asked: 'To what extent do you agree or disagree with the following statements?'

Legend: ■ Strongly agree □ Agree ▨ Disagree ▩ Strongly disagree ■ Don't know

Children are increasingly a danger to each other and to adults: 12% | 37% | 32% | 12% | 7%

British children are beginning to behave like animals: 16% | 38% | 31% | 11% | 5%

Something has to be done to protect us from children: 11% | 32% | 37% | 15% | 6%

People refer to children as feral but I don't think they behave this way: 7% | 35% | 34% | 11% | 13%

Sample size: 2021. Fieldwork: 14-16 October 2008. Source: YouGov (www.yougov.com)

Engaging communities in fighting crime

A high-powered team of Government officials spent eight months reviewing how crime affects communities in Britain. Here are ten key facts from the *Engaging communities in fighting crime* review

The author of the report, top civil servant Louise Casey, concludes: 'The public are not daft. They know what's wrong, they know what's right, and they know what they want on crime and justice. And it's time action was taken on their terms.'

Below we highlight ten key facts to come out of a series of consultations with members of the public, held as part of the *Engaging communities in fighting crime* review.

⇨ 55% of the public say crime is the most important issue facing Britain today.

Better parenting is the top thing (58%) the public say would do most to reduce crime

⇨ Only 33% of the public are confident that the Criminal Justice System meets the needs of

CabinetOffice

victims, but 79% agree it respects the rights of offenders.

⇨ 73% of the public say that hearing about someone being a victim of crime in their local area affects their feelings of safety and makes them cautious, angry and sad.

⇨ 91% of the public think the basic approaches and standards of service delivered by the police should be the same wherever they live.

⇨ Better parenting is the top thing (58%) the public say would do most to reduce crime and 58% of the public think that Friday night is the most important time for youth facilities to be available.

⇨ 90% of respondents to the review think the public are not told enough about what happens to those who have committed crime.

⇨ When asked what is the most important issue facing Britain on crime, the top answer from the public (29%) is that sentences are too lenient.

⇨ 90% of the public agree that community punishments for crime should involve some form of payback to the community.

⇨ When asked who they would trust as a source for national statistics on crime, the top answer from the public (48%) was an independent watchdog.

⇨ 75% of the public are prepared to play an active role in tackling crime.

June 2008

⇨ The above information is reprinted with kind permission from the Cabinet Office. Visit www.cabinetoffice.gov.uk for more information.

© *Crown copyright*

> ACTUALLY I'VE NEVER HAD ANY PROBLEMS IN THE COMMUNITY!

Crime, sentencing and your community

Sentencing explained

The sentencing process

When a crime is reported to the police, they will investigate it and try to identify a suspect. The police may arrest the suspect, or they may summon them to appear before a court.

When they have done so, they pass their evidence to the Crown Prosecution Service (CPS). A Crown Prosecutor decides whether there is enough evidence to prosecute, and whether it is in the public interest to do so.

When an offender appears in court and is convicted, magistrates and judges decide what the sentence they give should achieve. Their aims include:

⇨ punishment of the offender;

⇨ protection of the public;

⇨ reform, reparation and rehabilitation (which are explained opposite);

⇨ making amends to people affected by crime; and

⇨ reducing crime in the future.

Most criminal cases are dealt with by magistrates' courts, but the most serious cases go to Crown courts.

Sentencing options

Courts have a number of sentencing options to choose from. These fall into four bands:

⇨ discharges;

⇨ fines;

⇨ community sentences; and

⇨ prison.

Certain crimes carry automatic prison sentences. But in many cases, a sentence served in the community is more appropriate than a prison sentence. As well as punishing offenders, community sentences force offenders to think about the impact on their victim and about their reasons for committing the crime.

Offenders are to be found in every society and in every community. Their friends, neighbours, work colleagues and families can play a part in helping them to stop offending and become law-abiding citizens.

The sentence given by a court depends on how serious the crime is

Before deciding on the most appropriate sentence, the court will often ask the probation service to prepare a report on the offender to help them make the right decision. The sentencing decision is for the court – and no one else – and follows legal guidelines set out by the Sentencing Guidelines Council. However, judges and magistrates value the advice of probation staff who are skilled in assessing the risks posed by offenders and the work that needs to be done to help turn them away from crime.

The sentence may also depend on the offender's history – a first-time offender is unlikely to get the same sentence as someone who has committed offences in the past.

Discharges and fines are given for less serious crimes, Community Orders for more serious crimes, and prison for the most serious crimes of all.

Who gets which sentence?

The statistics in this section come from *Sentencing Statistics 2006, (England and Wales)*, published by the Ministry of Justice.

68% of offenders are fined

Nearly three-quarters of crimes that come to court are in the 'less serious' category. Most of these result in a fine. Fines work – evidence suggests that people who receive fines are no more likely to be convicted again than people who are sentenced in other ways. The payment rate for fines has improved from 55 per cent in 2002-03 to 83 per cent in 2005-06 (Source: Rebalancing the *Criminal Justice System*, July 2006).

13% of offenders are given community sentences

The Criminal Justice Act 2003 replaced the existing range of community sentences with a single Community Order which is made up of one or more possible requirements. The courts' choice of requirements means there is now much greater scope for imposing a sentence that best fits the circumstances of the case and the offender. What the offender is required to do depends on how serious the crime is and what the court decides is appropriate. The following pages explain Community Orders in more detail.

7% of people convicted of an offence receive a discharge

Even when an offender is found guilty, the court can decide that neither a community sentence nor a prison sentence would be appropriate. The offender still gets a

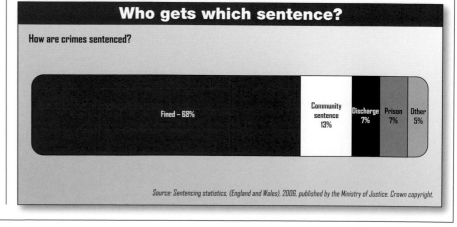

Who gets which sentence?

How are crimes sentenced?

Fined – 68% | Community sentence 13% | Discharge 7% | Prison 7% | Other 5%

Source: Sentencing statistics, (England and Wales), 2006, published by the Ministry of Justice. Crown copyright.

criminal record, so they haven't 'got away' with a crime.

A discharge can be 'absolute' or 'conditional'

An absolute discharge means that no further action is taken. Either the offence was very minor, or the court considers that the experience has been enough.

A conditional discharge means that the offender receives no immediate punishment. However, if they commit another offence within a certain period (up to three years), the court can punish them for the original offence as well as for the new one.

Other financial penalties

⇨ Compensation: If someone is convicted, they can be ordered to pay money to their victim through the court.

⇨ Fixed penalty notices: These are given by the police for less serious offences, such as illegal parking or public disorder offences. If people who get fixed penalties pay within the time allowed, they won't have to go to court and risk getting a criminal record.

Anti-Social Behaviour Orders (ASBOs)

In addition to criminal sentences, ASBOs are civil orders given by magistrates' courts. They aim to protect communities by restricting individuals whose behaviour is intimidating or causes problems in their community.

If someone breaks the terms of their ASBO, they may be committing a criminal offence and will be punished accordingly.

7% of offenders are sentenced to prison

The Criminal Justice Act 2003 made significant changes to prison sentences in England and Wales.

Most offenders who go to prison receive sentences of less than 12 months.

Less than one-third of offenders who go to prison are given sentences of 12 months or more. Most offenders who have been given these sentences can be released halfway through their sentence, but they will remain on licence – under probation service supervision – in the community for the whole of the rest of their sentence.

Dangerous offenders will receive either:

⇨ an Extended Sentence for Public Protection, with no automatic early release and a longer period on licence; or

⇨ an Indeterminate Sentence, which means the offender will only be released when it is safe to do so.

A very small proportion of offenders (0.5 per cent) receive life sentences.

What is a Community Order?

The Community Order is a sentence served in the community which replaces a range of earlier community sentences. It was introduced in April 2005 and is available to the courts for offences committed from that time onwards. The offender continues to live in the community but must follow the requirements of the Order.

There are 12 requirements available and a Community Order will include one or more of them. The requirements used will differ from case to case according to the individual offender and the offence committed. For example, a Community Order passed on an offender who got into a fight because he drank too much will differ from an Order passed on someone who stole from shops to help fund a drug addiction.

It is very important that the courts pass the right sentence for the offender because this can make a big difference to whether they go on to commit more crimes.

Being tough on offenders

Offenders can be ordered to comply with one or more of a range of requirements as part of a Community Order.

Like prison sentences, Community Orders are used to punish as well as reform and rehabilitate offenders and are not a soft option. They also provide the opportunity in some cases for offenders to make amends to the victims of their crimes.

⇨ They vary in severity according to the individual offender and the crime committed.

⇨ They deliver justice by combining a suitable punishment for the offender, sometimes with reparation – either by getting offenders to put something back into their community or make amends directly to the victim of their crime.

⇨ They can play a major part in rehabilitating an offender. They make offenders face up to and deal with problems that might be causing them to commit crime – like drug abuse – and challenge them to change their behaviour. A rehabilitated criminal is less likely to offend again.

This all means that sentences can be tailored to respond to individual offences and offenders, increasing the chances of them developing a life away from crime.

Offenders can be ordered to do one or more of a range of requirements as part of a Community Order

Unpaid work

This involves demanding and constructive activities, such as conservation work, cleaning up graffiti, or working with a local charity. The local community also benefits. An offender will have to carry out between 40 and 300 hours of compulsory unpaid work.

Activity

Participation in specified activities may include an offender improving their basic skills (such as reading and writing) or making reparation to the people affected by the crime.

Programmes

Nationally approved programmes are designed with the aim of changing an offender's behaviour. For example, an offender found guilty of drink-driving may be required to undertake a specific drink-driving programme.

Prohibited activity

An offender may be ordered not to do certain activities at specified times.

Curfews

An offender may be ordered to stay at a particular location, usually their home, for certain hours of the day. Curfews help to structure an offender's life and break the cycle of offending. They will normally have to wear an electronic tag during their sentence.

Exclusion

An offender may be prohibited from certain areas for up to two years.

Residence

An offender may be required to live in a specified place, such as an approved hostel or other residential accommodation.

Mental health treatment

After taking professional medical advice, the court may decide that the offender's sentence should include mental health treatment. The offender must consent to this treatment.

Drug rehabilitation

If an offender commits crime as a result of a drug addiction, and if they consent to treatment, they may be required to go on a drug rehabilitation programme. The programme will last for between six months and three years and may involve monthly reviews of the offender's progress.

Alcohol treatment

This requirement is suitable for offenders whose crime may be linked to alcohol abuse. An offender must agree to the treatment and it must last for at least six months.

Supervision

This requirement means that work is done specifically to promote the offender's rehabilitation. It is different from simply ensuring that the offender complies with the Order. This requirement is often used with other requirements, such as Activity and Programmes, to ensure that progress made is supported and followed up.

Attendance centre

Offenders under the age of 25 may be required to attend a particular place (perhaps a village hall or a school out of hours), where they must participate in constructive activities, at a specified time for between 12 and 36 hours, over the course of their sentence.

Better sentences mean less crime

Suspended Sentence Orders

In some cases a court may decide that a short (under 12 months) prison sentence is required but that it is not necessary for the offender to be sent to prison straight away. In such cases the court will impose a Suspended Sentence Order in which the prison element of the sentence is suspended for between six months and two years. In this period the court will set requirements, drawn from the list of 12 available for the Community Order, which the offender must comply with during the period of suspension. If they comply, they will not go to prison for the offences. If they break any of the requirements of the Order, they will be returned to court and may be sent to prison to serve all or part of the prison element of their sentence.

⇨ Prisoners who aren't considered dangerous, and who are serving sentences of 12 months or more, will be released halfway through their sentence. But they will continue to be on licence until the end of their sentence. This means that if they break the conditions of their licence or commit another crime, they will be returned to prison immediately.

⇨ Prisons are not only about punishing offenders – the Prison Service works to help rehabilitate offenders. For example, offenders in prison can study for qualifications or may be involved in workshop projects that can help them to get a job once they are released.

Protecting the public

Offenders living in the community who are considered to be potentially dangerous are closely monitored. They may have completed a prison sentence and be in the community on licence or they may not have committed offences serious enough to have been sent to prison.

⇨ Criminal Justice agencies work with other organisations, such as health authorities, to monitor offenders who have committed violent and sexual crimes.

⇨ Police, probation, prison and other agencies meet regularly under the Multi-Agency Public Protection Arrangements (MAPPA) to assess the risks posed by specific serious offenders and set up joint plans to manage them. New public protection prison sentences were introduced in April 2005 as part of the Criminal Justice Act 2003. They provide even greater powers for courts to ensure that offenders they consider to be too dangerous to be out in the community stay in prison for longer.

The chance of being a victim of crime is currently at its lowest since the British Crime Survey began in 1981.

The risk of becoming a victim has fallen from 40 per cent in 1995-96 to 23 per cent in 2005-06. In fact, 74 per cent of crime falls into the 'least serious' category, and public confidence in the Criminal Justice System is increasing.

Working together to manage offenders

Managing offenders is important, whether they are in prison, serving a community sentence or on licence from prison.

The National Offender Management Service (NOMS) brings together the work of correctional services to focus on end-to-end management of the offender.

NOMS covers a number of organisations, including prisons and probation, to ensure that a range of services is available to adult offenders and to those on remand throughout England and Wales. It is also working in alliance with organisations in the corporate, civic and faith, voluntary and community sectors to assist in its aim of reducing re-offending.

Offenders are monitored and supported through the punishment, reparation and rehabilitation processes. The police, NOMS and other organisations, such as health and housing services, may continue to have a role even after the offender's sentence has been completed.

This support helps to protect the public and aims to ensure that reoffending is reduced.

The courts work with the police so that offenders who are given fines pay them as ordered.

There are many opportunities for volunteers and mentors to assist in work to help offenders turn away from crime. To find out how you can work with different Criminal Justice agencies, visit www.ccjf.org/what/index.html

May 2008

⇨ The above information is an extract from the document *Crime sentencing and your community* and is reprinted with kind permission from the Criminal Justice System. Visit www.cjsonline.gov.uk for more information.

© *Criminal Justice System*

Community sentencing

Community sentences are a demanding punishment and include several different requirements that focus on helping rehabilitate the offender and stop them from committing more crime. They are flexible, so that each sentence is designed to address the particular offender and the causes of their offending behaviour

The purpose of community sentencing

Community sentences have three important functions:

⇨ they punish offenders for their crimes with hard work and tough curfews that take away free time;

⇨ they benefit society by making offenders do hard work in the community for no pay, to 'pay back' for the damage they have caused;

⇨ they play a role in stopping offenders committing more crimes by identifying why a person commits crimes and providing programmes and treatments to stop it happening again;

Community sentences are able to both punish and reform offenders

Community sentences are able to both punish and reform offenders because they have 12 possible requirements. The judge or magistrates choose a combination of requirements for each offender which is intended to punish them and give them an opportunity to change.

The 12 requirements of a community sentence

The judge or magistrates consider what the offender has done, why they did it and how likely they are to commit another crime. They then decide on the number and type of requirements the offender gets.

The 12 requirements are:

⇨ Community Payback – anything between 40 and 300 hours of unpaid work, for the benefit of the community;

⇨ a compulsory activity – such as attending a drug centre, or completing an education or basic skills course;

⇨ a programme to address particular behaviour – such as violence, drug or alcohol abuse, domestic violence or drink-driving;

⇨ a prohibited activity – a ban on an activity such as going to a pub or attending a football match;

⇨ a curfew – monitored by an electronic tag;

⇨ exclusion – a ban from entering a particular place for up to two years;

⇨ residence – having to live at a specified place, such as a probation hostel or private address;

⇨ mental health treatment;

⇨ drug rehabilitation;

⇨ alcohol treatment;

⇨ supervision – attending regular appointments with a probation officer to work on changing attitudes and behaviour;

⇨ going to an Attendance Centre, where 18-24-year-olds can address their offending behaviour.

What happens when offenders break the rules

If an offender breaks the rules of their community order, they are sent back to court and given a bigger penalty. In some cases, this will mean being re-sentenced and sent to prison.

⇨ The above information is reprinted with kind permission from Directgov. Visit www.direct.gov.uk for more information on this and other related issues.

© Crown copyright

More offenders serve community punishments

Record numbers of people serving punishments in the community

A report published today by the Centre for Crime and Justice Studies at King's College London reveals that record numbers of people are serving court orders in the community.

The report, published by the Centre for Crime and Justice Studies at King's College London, highlights that in 2007, 162,648 people started court orders in the community, the highest ever recorded number. It represents a 36 per cent increase in the decade since 1997. The orders include both community sentences and Suspended Sentence Orders.

The *Community Sentences Digest* report states: 'Prison overcrowding is a well-known fact. What is less well known is that community sentence caseloads are also overcrowded. The effect is far less graphic than images of overcrowded jails but the impact is equally damaging.'

The report notes that the ratio of offenders to qualified probation officers has risen from 31:1 to 40:1, with staff supervising caseloads which are, on average, much larger than those of practitioners in youth offending teams. It also highlights high sickness levels amongst the probation workforce. In 2007-08, the average number of sick days for each employee was 12.1, one of the highest in the public sector.

'Far more community sentences are given out each year than prison sentences'

Helen Mills, the project lead on Community Sentences at the Centre for Crime and Justice Studies, said:

'The *Digest* shows three years on from their introduction, half of the requirements which can be issued with community sentences are rarely used. Given a key part of the government's community sentences agenda is that orders should be tailored to meet sentence purpose and individual need, their limited use should pose serious questions for the Ministry of Justice.'

Richard Garside, Director of the Centre for Crime and Justice Studies, added:

'Community sentences are one of the main ways the state imposes punishment on those convicted of offences. Indeed far more community sentences are given out each year than prison sentences. Over the past decade community sentences have grown alongside the rise in the prison population. This places in some doubt the regular claim that their increased use can be an effective means of controlling the growth in prison.'
25 November 2008

⇨ The above information is reprinted with kind permission from the Centre for Crime and Justice Studies. Visit www.crimeandjustice.org.uk for more information.

© King's College London

Offenders to wear high-visibility jackets

Information from the Ministry of Justice

B randed high-visibility jackets must be worn by offenders carrying out work on community payback projects from today as part of a government drive to ensure the public can see punishment being carried out in the community.

The roll-out of the new jackets across England and Wales builds on a recommendation from Louise Casey's review, *Engaging communities in fighting crime*, published in June this year outlining the importance of people seeing justice being done.

Launching the jackets, Secretary of State for Justice Jack Straw said:

'Community punishments like unpaid work can be more productive than prison in getting offenders to stop their criminality. But public confidence in these punishments is lower than it should be, not least because they are less visible than they should be.

'The public, the taxpayer, has an absolute right to know what unpaid work is being done to pay back to them for the wrongs the offender has committed. These high-visibility jackets with the distinctive logo "community payback" are one way in which I am trying to open up this part of the criminal justice system.'

Jack Straw has asked Louise Casey to identify more ways to make the justice system more visible, specifically offenders paying for their crimes in the community.

Courts are now able to hand out tougher and more intense penalties for a range of offenders who are ordered to carry out work such as picking up litter, renovating community centres, clearing undergrowth and graffiti for local communities.

Home Secretary Jacqui Smith said:

'Making sure that people feel safe and secure in their communities is my top priority. And central to that is building people's confidence that crime is being tackled in their areas and justice is being done – and being seen to be done.

'The new high-visibility jackets for Community Payback are another step in helping to build community confidence in the criminal justice system.'

Neighbourhood, Crime and Justice Adviser Louise Casey said:

'I am pleased that the Government is taking the views of the public seriously. It is a step towards building the public's confidence in the criminal justice system – that it is on their side – and not solely on the side of the offender. This is not about humiliation – it's about ensuring the public can see justice being done. It's about letting the public know that there are consequences for committing crime, that Community Payback is not a "slap on the wrist" and that they can see how it can benefit their local area.

'The more confidence the public have in the system, the more we can ask the public to play their part – by reporting crime, giving evidence in court and supporting victims in their community.

'I will rise to the challenge set me by the Justice Secretary to make sure that Community Payback is visible to local communities right across the country.'

Recent statistics show that frequency of reoffending for community sentences has fallen sharply by 13%. That's why in March the Ministry of Justice announced £40m to further support the probation service, so that magistrates have at their disposal tough community sentences that will punish offenders.

1 December 2008

⇨ The above information is reprinted with kind permission from the Ministry of Justice. Visit www.justice.gov.uk for more information on this and other related topics.

Going ballistic

Dealing with guns, gangs and knives

Murders involving knives and firearms, such as the cases of the headteacher Philip Lawrence, who was stabbed by a teenager while trying to protect a pupil, or seven-year-old Toni-Ann Byfield, shot in the back by a drug dealer in a North London bedsit, never fail to grab the headlines, yet they are relatively rare. Gun crime represents only 0.4% of all recorded crime in England and Wales.[1,2]

By Dr Bob Golding and Jonathan McClory

The public are often sceptical, however, when they read figures such as this – and they have reason to be so. Official police statistics and the annual British Crime Survey do not offer a complete picture of gun and knife crime because much of it – especially violence between criminals and offences by children under 16 – goes unreported. Organisations that could provide extra data to fill out the picture, such as the Ministry of Defence or hospital A&E departments, are often reluctant to do so. And the Government sometimes uses minor variations from one year to another to present a misleading picture of an improving situation. In other words, our crime figures do not reflect the experiences of many communities in England and Wales. This conflict between official statistics and public opinion forms the backdrop to this report.

The authors, Dr Bob Golding, a former assistant chief constable, and Jonathan McClory, have worked from the point of view of those closest to gun and knife crime – the public and frontline workers. They review the latest research on gangs and the illegal use of firearms and also draw on their own surveys of young offenders; police constables and sergeants; two detailed case studies consisting of interviews with senior police officers; managers of youth offending teams (YOTs); and specially commissioned public opinion polling. Secondary sources taken from Youth Justice Board statistics, Home Office and British Crime Survey statistics and police strategy documents supplement this material.

The incomplete official picture of firearms crime and the timelag of up to two years in publishing crime figures make it difficult for the Government to identify or respond promptly to emerging trends. The evidence collected for this report suggests that chaotic, street-level firearm offences, often associated with young people, have risen:

⇨ Nearly three-quarters of police constables and sergeants believe that gang crime has become worse over the past five years;[3]

⇨ More than half of young offenders feel that the police are unable to protect them from violent crime in their area and eight out of ten people in Britain think violent youth crime is worse now than it was five years ago;[4]

⇨ More than half of young offenders have had a gun or knife used against them or been threatened with a gun or knife in the past 12 months;[5]

Nearly three-quarters of police constables and sergeants believe that gang crime has become worse over the past five years

---

⇨ More than one in four of those surveyed (27%) have either been the victim of a violent crime committed by children or young people, have had a gun or knife used against them, have been threatened with one or know a friend or relative who has had a gun or knife used against them or who has been threatened with one in the past 12 months;[6]

⇨ One in five people between the ages of 19 and 24 know a friend or family member who has had a gun or knife used against them or been threatened with a gun or knife in the past year.[7]

This perceived rise in violence among young people, frequently involving guns or other weapons and not linked to financial motives, has drawn attention to changes in the culture of gangs. These once stable groupings that existed to protect illegal commodities now seem to be more volatile; their members younger and highly territorial. There is anecdotal evidence from gang members themselves that young people in deprived areas deliberately join criminal gangs for personal protection. They want to be armed because they believe that others are armed.

The authors agree with the Home Office that the main threat from firearms at gang and street level is presented by legally purchased imitation and deactivated weapons that are then illegally converted to fire live ammunition. Some of these firearms sell for as little as £50 and a single firearm can circulate over many years within and between criminal groups. Although this trend has been apparent for some time, the necessary amendments to existing gun laws have not yet been put into place.

Legislation is a mess. Laws governing offensive weapons are derived from at least six separate Acts, introduced piecemeal since 1968. There is no legal framework dealing with knives and offensive weapons as a whole, while wider measures such as the Criminal Justice and the Anti-Social Behaviour Acts 2003 also contain provisions relating to firearms. Every new provision inevitably increases the chance that the police will make mistakes that result in a failed prosecution – arresting a suspect under the wrong section of an Act, for example.

Golding and McClory make more than 20 recommendations, divided into four categories: information and funding; supply; demand; and law reform. These will be developed and fully costed for the second book in this series, to be published in the autumn.

Notes

1 Hales G, Lewis C and Silverstone D, *Gun Crime: the market in and use of illegal firearms*, Home Office Research Study 298, 2006

2 Coleman C, Hird C and Povey D, *Violent Crime Overview, homicide and gun crime 2004/5*, Home Office RDS, 2006

3 Policy Exchange polling

4 Policy Exchange polling

5 Policy Exchange polling

6 YouGov polling for Policy Exchange

7 YouGov polling for Policy Exchange

1 July 2008

⇨ The above information is reprinted with kind permission from Policy Exchange. Visit www.policyexchange.org.uk for more information on this and other related topics.

© Policy Exchange

Restorative justice

Information from the Youth Justice Board

If you are a victim of a crime, you may be offered the chance to take part in a restorative justice (RJ) process. This provides the opportunity for those directly affected by an offence - victim, offender and members of the community - to communicate and agree how to deal with the offence and its consequences.

Restorative processes typically result in the offender making practical amends (reparation) to repair the harm - this may include an apology. Communication between victim and offender can help victims put the offence behind them and be more satisfied with the outcome.

The consultation document, *Developing Restorative Justice: An Action Plan*, was published in November 2006 and sets out proposed actions to be carried out to promote effective restorative justice practices.

RJ is an important part of youth justice orders and sentences, from Final Warnings and Referral Orders to Reparation Orders, Action Plan Orders and Supervision Orders. The best known and most commonly used restorative processes are:

Victim/offender mediation

The victim and offender, helped by an independent person, communicate with one another. This may be by direct meeting or, if preferred by either the victim or the offender, indirectly with the third person acting as 'go between' in a 'shuttle mediation'. Questions may be asked, information exchanged and an agreement reached.

Restorative conferencing

Supporters, as well as victim and offender, meet together in a conference run by a trained person. At the end, agreements are made that set out what the offender will do to deal with the harm done.

Family group conferencing

The young person who has offended, with members of his/her extended family, meet with the victim and supporters of the victim and possibly representatives of agencies, e.g. social services and schools. The meeting is run by an independent third person and after all views have been stated, the family have a private meeting time to create a plan, which is then put to the whole conference for acceptance.

Referral Order Youth Offender Panels

First-time convicted young offenders and parents meet with trained community volunteer panel members to discuss the offence and its consequences and agree a contract to repair the harm and address the causes of offending behaviour. Victims may be invited to attend if they wish, or have their views put before the panel.

Reparation

Reparation is a practical way to pay back for the harm caused by the offence, either by directly repairing the harm or through constructive work to help the local community. The victim is usually consulted about what should be done. Reparation can include:

Reparation to the victim

For example, an oral or written apology, or financial or supervised activity-based reparation to the victim.

Community reparation

Includes a variety of activities to 'pay back' benefits to the community, including work similar to community service activity.

⇨ The above information is re-printed with kind permission from the Youth Justice Board for England and Wales. Visit www.yjb.gov.uk for more information.
© *Youth Justice Board for England and Wales*

The danger of Tasers

At some point we will begin to wonder how it was such a monstrous weapon was given to the police with so little debate

Looking at the photographs of the killer of Rhys Jones, Sean Mercer and his fellow gang members, it's not difficult to imagine why police want to acquire the DNA of such people as early as possible in their lives. Nor is it difficult to see why they want access to 10,000 Taser guns, or why they are mounting operations in Kent and Lambeth to photograph children for a database even though the have not been found guilty of any crime.

To most people these responses seem proportionate to the epidemic of gang crime and anti-social behaviour on Britain's troubled housing estates. The public is tired of the violence and yobbish behaviour and want it stopped. Though understandable, this impatience fills Jacqui Smith's sails and is one of the chief factors in the general attack on rights and liberties undertaken by Labour since 1997.

The European Court of Human Rights unanimously decided that the retention of innocent people's DNA breached Article 8 of the Human Rights Act. Yesterday the home secretary responded with a speech that appeared - but only if you have the mental age of five - to make concessions to that judgement. She said that children under the age of ten would be removed from the database, but not those were under ten when their DNA was taken from them.

This involves about 70 children. At the same time she announced a white paper on forensics and that she was considering a move to take DNA samples from everyone sent to jail before the National DNA database was started.

The very small number of children now to be taken off the DNA database is a rather cynical gesture designed to reassure people that the government is responsive to the demands of its own legislation – the Human Rights Act. If there were any real concern about the rights of young children, the police would not now be using the sinister FITs – Forward Intelligence Teams – to photograph them. As we learned in a court case the other day, FITs are already breaching the rights of demonstrators by collecting and storing images of people who legitimately attend demonstrations and protests (Article 11 of the Human Rights Act). Now they are deployed in officially sanctioned operations against children.

We may find ourselves saying that these children are out of control and something has to be done – and that is right – but to allow the police to experiment by building archives of mug shots and film of young people who have not been found guilty of any crime is to back arbitrary and unlawful harassment. It is oppressive and a dangerous precedent.

Labour has been very astute in creating an atmosphere of fear and hatred of young people but without conceding that so many of the problems – gang membership, the lack of social cohesion and general lassitude and fecklessness in blighted inner city areas – have all increased under this government. An absence of intelligent social policy, or simply neglect, is in almost every case followed by oppressive legislation and the kind of ad hoc measures that you see in Kent and Lambeth. These things go uncriticised because the tabloid press feeds on the same hatred and fears.

This is how Jacqui Smith has been able to give the police 10,000 Tasers with very little fuss. As Amnesty International reports, these weapons are lethal. They discharge 50,000 volts and have been responsible for the death of 344 Americans between 2001 and August 2008. 'The problem with Tasers is that they are inherently open to abuse, as they are easy to carry and easy to use and can inflict severe pain at the push of a button, without leaving substantial marks,' said the author of Amnesty's report Angela Wright. Many people were shot with the gun after failing to comply with a police command, and that I suspect is exactly how it will be deployed in Britain. At some point we will begin to wonder how it was such a monstrous weapon was given to the police with so little debate.

17 December 2008

Thousands of new Tasers for the police

Information from the Home Office

Police forces in England and Wales will receive more than 6,000 new Tasers, the Home Secretary announced recently.

The roll-out across England and Wales to extend the use of Tasers to specially trained police response officers followed a successful trial in ten forces.

Home Office Scientific Development Branch monitored the use of the Tasers in the ten trial forces. Statistics showed that of the 661 recorded uses of Tasers, 85% involved the weapon just being drawn, aimed, arced or the subject being 'red-dotted' – showing the Taser's powerful deterrent effect and its benefits in preventing any escalation in violence. Tasers were only discharged in 93 of the 661 uses.

The roll-out of Taser followed earlier reports from HOSDB and the Association of Chief Police Officers. Their findings stated that Tasers provided real benefits for both public and police officer safety in incidents involving serious violence.

Jacqui Smith said, 'I am proud that we have one of the few police services around the world that do not regularly carry firearms and I want to keep it that way.

'Every day the police put themselves in danger to protect us, the public. They deserve our support, so I want to give the police the tools they tell me they need to confront dangerous people. That is why I have given every police force the number of Tasers they have requested.

'I am pleased that police forces up and down the country have used the additional funding I made available for Tasers.'

24 March 2009

⇨ The above information is reprinted with kind permission from the Home Office. Visit www.homeoffice.gov.uk for more information.

'Reclaim the streets' plea by new think-tank report

Major shift in police culture needed to allay fears about yobbish behaviour

Police officers should be instructed to reclaim the streets for the law-abiding majority by waging a concerted campaign against anti-social behaviour, according to a landmark new report from the think-tank set up by the former Conservative leader Iain Duncan Smith.

The Centre for Social Justice report, produced by a working group chaired by Ray Mallon, an elected mayor and former senior policeman, cites new polling showing that the public regard confronting rowdy and abusive behaviour as the top priority for law enforcement officers.

They also overwhelmingly support a greater and more visible police presence on the streets.

According to an exclusive YouGov poll commissioned by the CSJ working group, 76 per cent of people think that the police are intervening 'too little' against anti-social behaviour.

And 72 per cent think 'it is never acceptable' for an on-duty police officer not to intervene when they have observed a crime or a threat to public safety.

Yet the rules of engagement for most of Britain's 140,000 police officers stop them exercising their judgement about when to intervene to bring troublemakers to heel. The so-called 'arrest or ignore' culture prevalent in modern policing and a suffocating and time-consuming level of bureaucracy mean that officers frequently walk on by rather than act to curb unruly youths.

An arrest typically takes a constable away from the beat for seven hours and the average full-time police officer is on patrol for only seven hours a week. In order for the police to add one full-time officer to street patrol, five new officers need to be employed.

The report *A Force to be Reckoned With* says that police should once again be granted the discretion to issue a metaphorical slap on the wrist to wrongdoers guilty of minor but intimidating infringements such as street drinking, begging, dropping litter and petty vandalism.

---

76 per cent of people think that the police are intervening 'too little' against anti-social behaviour

---

It says that police should be organised into 'Interventionist Neighbourhood Teams' and placed under a duty to act whenever they observe a crime or anti-social behaviour, though not always to make an arrest.

The report also endorses a 'crackdown and consolidation' approach to law enforcement in high-crime areas.

'In areas characterised by social breakdown (with prevalent drug and alcohol misuse, high rates of family breakdown and concentration of at-risk children), short-term police crackdowns can create space for other agencies to move in and address the problems underlying crime,' it says.

In the wake of public outrage over incidents where police officers have cited health and safety rules as a justification for failing to act in life-threatening situations, the report says they should be under orders to put themselves 'in harm's way' if the safety of the public is at risk. The report commends Surrey police for instituting such a policy and says it should be implemented across the country.

Ray Mallon, the elected independent mayor of Middlesborough, who has 28 years experience as a police officer and who reached the rank of detective superintendent, chaired the eight-strong working group who produced the report. The group

includes two former chief constables, Steve Green of Nottinghamshire and Sir Charles Pollard of Thames Valley.

As detective inspector in Hartlepool in the mid-1990s (one of Cleveland's four policing divisions), his brand of 'Here and Now' policing based on the four principles of education, prevention, punishment and rehabilitation, led to a 43 per cent fall in overall crime and led to him being christened 'Robocop' by the national media.

Mr Mallon said: 'The British public want the police to reclaim the streets for the law-abiding majority. All our polling shows that. Serious crime such as robbery, burglary and violence is far too high and must be addressed further. However, what people really worry about is anti-social behaviour. That affects everyone almost every day across large parts of the country, whereas serious crime intrudes far less often.

'But we will not make any headway in restoring order and civility to our streets without a fundamental change in the culture of policing. Officers should be trusted once more to decide if a breach of the law merits a firm word with a troublemaker or whether an arrest is necessary. Centrally determined targets are not the way to determine the course of 21st-century policing.

'Above all, I want the police to become a force to be reckoned with.'

Mr Duncan Smith said: 'I want us to learn from New York, where active neighbourhood policing has made such a spectacular difference. We want to get the police out on the streets, where they're needed.

'It's a complete waste for them to be in the office...We need police who aren't afraid of policing the streets – a police culture that treats the streets as their office. Police need to know they can take the necessary risks and use their discretion, and that they'll be supported by politicians and the public if things go wrong.'

Other key recommendations in the report include:
⇨ Scrapping most of the national police targets which have distorted police priorities and led to the situation where officers often fail to respond to public concerns about crime and low-level disorder.
⇨ Restore to the police the right to prosecute for minor crimes.
⇨ Greater operational independence of chief constables – for instance they should no longer be subject to fixed-term appointments.

29 March 2009

⇨ The above information is reprinted with kind permission from the Centre for Social Justice. Visit www.centreforsocialjustice.org.uk for more information on this and other related topics.

© *Centre for Social Justice*

Stop and search

Information from HeadsUp

Stop and search powers allow the police to combat street crime and anti-social behaviour, and prevent more serious crimes. Stop and search is when the police stop someone and ask them what they are doing, where they are going, what they are carrying, etc. They may also search that person if they are not happy with their response to the questions.

What happens if I'm stopped and searched?

If you are stopped you'll first be asked where you're going and what you've been doing. The police may then decide to search you but only if they have a good reason; for example, that you fit the profile of a criminal seen in the area, or they think you're acting suspiciously.

Here is what should happen if you are stopped and searched by the police:
⇨ the search will take place on the street;
⇨ if the officer asks you to remove more than your coat and gloves, or anything you wear for religious reasons, they must take you somewhere out of public view;
⇨ you'll be asked to turn out your pockets and show the officers the contents of your bag;
⇨ they can also search your vehicle, even if you aren't present, but they must leave a notice to say what they've done;
⇨ if you're carrying something illegal, such as a weapon, or the police believe you've committed a crime, you may be arrested;
⇨ if they don't find anything, your details will be recorded for monitoring purposes, and you'll be allowed to go.

You don't have to give your name, address or date of birth to the police if you're stopped and searched unless you're being reported for an offence. However, the police will ask you your ethnic origin.

Stop and searches affect black and ethnic minority communities more than white people. If you are black you are seven times more likely to be stopped and if you're Asian twice as likely to be stopped. This is why a lot of people are against stop and search powers because they think it is discriminating against non-white people and this is why the police must ask the ethnic origin of people they stop, so that they have a record.

The officer will fill out a form outlining the reason for stopping you, the outcome of the stop and search and their name, and give you a copy. This information won't be held on file against you unless you're charged with an offence.

February 2009

⇨ The above information is reprinted with kind permission from HeadsUp. Visit www.headsup.org.uk for more information.

© *Hansard Society*

Rights on arrest

When a police officer makes an arrest, he or she is taking you under the care and control of the law

This means that for the time being you lose certain freedoms, such as to go and do as you please... but in return you are given certain rights which protect you against unreasonable treatment. As soon as you are arrested, you have the right to know why you have been arrested.

At the police station you are entitled to:

⇨ See a solicitor free of charge;
⇨ Have someone told where you are;
⇨ Read a copy of the Codes of Practice, which explains the procedures the police should follow in such circumstances;
⇨ You should be given a written note of these rights and cautioned.

You can be detained by the police only if they do not have enough evidence to charge you and they have good reason to believe that they can obtain further evidence by continuing with your detention.

You cannot normally be held for more than 24 hours without being charged or released. If a serious offence is being investigated, a senior police officer can authorise your detention for a further 12 hours,

which can be extended up to a total of 96 hours, but only with the approval of a magistrates' court.

Questioning

If you are under 17, you should usually not be interviewed by the police without a parent or appropriate adult present (an appropriate adult is someone who knows you, such as an adult friend or teacher). You must give the police your name and address but you have the right after that to stay silent. If you do not answer further questions and the case goes to trial, the court will be told of this and your failure to answer questions may strengthen the case against you. If you fail to answer questions in court, the magistrates or jury are allowed to take this into account in deciding whether you are guilty.

There are clear rules which govern the way in which a police officer can question a person, designed to stop unfair pressure being placed on a suspect. There should be regular breaks for food, the cell and interview room should be clean and properly heated, and the police should not follow a line of questioning which puts unreasonable pressure on the suspect. Someone who is deaf or has difficulty in understanding English should be given a signer or an interpreter.

If you are arrested, the police must give you written information about your legal rights when you arrive at the police station.

Legal advice

Whether you are arrested or go to a police station voluntarily, you are entitled to free legal advice from a solicitor who will advise you while you are being questioned. If you have been arrested or are being questioned about a serious arrestable offence or if you feel at all unsure about your legal position, it is better not to answer questions (except your name and address) until you have had a chance to speak to the solicitor.

If the police are investigating a very serious offence they can, with the approval of a senior officer, delay access to a solicitor on the grounds that talking to a solicitor might interfere with the evidence, alert other suspects or hinder the recovery of stolen property.

Tape recording

Your interview at the police station will probably be recorded on tape. It will begin with questions about your name and address before moving on to more serious matters.

If your interview is not recorded, notes should be made by the officer concerned. You should have the opportunity to see these notes and to sign them if you agree they are a fair record of what was said.

Fingerprints and photographs

The police can take your fingerprints if they have reason to suspect your involvement in a crime. They are also allowed to take your photograph, but cannot force you to have your picture taken against your will (until you are charged or cautioned). The Serious Organised Crime and Police Act 2005 states that police have the power to retain all fingerprints and photographs of people arrested, even if they are subsequently released without charge or later acquitted.

The caution

Once a police officer has reason to believe that you have committed an offence, he or she must caution you by explaining that it may harm your defence if you do not mention when questioned something which you later rely on in court. Anything you do say may be given in evidence.

After questioning you, the police must decide what to do next. If there appears to be enough evidence, they can:

⇨ Charge you with the offence;

⇨ Send the papers to the Crown Prosecution Service, for them to decide whether to charge;

⇨ Arrange to issue you with a formal caution.

This is a strong warning from a senior police officer reminding you that you could have been sent to court, and that if you commit further offences, that is almost certainly what will happen. Formal cautions are given more often now because the re-offence rate is lower amongst those who do not go to court, but a caution can be given only if the person admits guilt.

If the police feel there is not enough evidence to make a charge, they will either decide to take no further action (and the case against you will be dropped), or will delay any decision while further enquiries are made.

Charge

When you are charged with an offence you are given a charge sheet, containing details of the offence of which you are charged, when and where you are due to appear in court and the conditions of your bail.

Once you are charged you should not usually be asked any further questions unless, perhaps, new information has come to light.

Bail

If you are charged with an offence the law states that you should normally be released on bail – unless the police doubt the truth of the name or address you have given or believe you should be held for the protection of yourself or others, or it is felt that you are unlikely to turn up in court if released.

If the police do not release you, you must be brought before a magistrate, at the earliest opportunity, who will decide whether you can be released on bail, and if so, what conditions should apply. For example, you may be required to report to the police station once a week, or to have someone provide a financial guarantee that you will be present in court when required.

Bail cannot be given to anyone charged with murder, attempted murder, rape or attempted rape who already has a conviction for one of these serious offences. Courts also need not grant bail if it appears that the defendant was already on bail when the offence was committed.

This information is from *YCP*, a pocket-sized guide to the law. It provides useful legal advice and information about many of the situations you may encounter. For further information please contact the Citizenship Foundation on 020 7367 0500.

⇨ The above information is reprinted with kind permission from TheSite. Visit www.thesite.org for more information.

© *TheSite*

How ASBOs help

The case studies below are just some real-life examples of cases in which ASBOs have been successful in bringing respite to communities

Shirley Fenn from Mansfield, Nottingham

Shirley's community was experiencing serious anti-social behaviour perpetrated by two boys whose family moved in next door to her three years ago. Their outrageous behaviour included holding all-night parties in the street leaving residents gardens filled with debris and vomit, damage to property and harassment and threatening behaviour.

Shirley contacted local councillors and her MP to set up a meeting with fellow residents to discuss what action the community could take. Shirley provided the council with information, encouraged ten witnesses to give statements and supported them through court hearings.

As a result of Shirley's actions, two anti-social behaviour orders (ASBOs) and a parenting order were granted against the family.

Shirley explained that one of the youths who received the ASBOs did initially treat it as a badge of honour. However, when he breached it and had to go to court where he was told he would face a custodial sentence if he breached again, he realised just how serious the implications were. The anti-social behaviour caused by the young men has been dramatically reduced and life on Shirley's street has improved immeasurably.

Lynda King Taylor, London

Lynda King Taylor is Chair of the Paddington Police Community Sector Working Group. The problems faced by Lynda and her community included noisy prostitutes and their aggressive pimps who were making life in the area a misery with foul language, excessive drug taking, sexual indecency and constant harassment and shouting obscenities, which was taking its toll on the residents. Lynda helped service the first ASBO awarded in Westminster for aggressive vice, which brought much needed respite to the community in Paddington. The group were recently successful in securing two further ASBOs on aggressive prostitutes who had been plaguing the residents of Sussex Gardens and the surrounding streets.

Lynda told us: 'We could never have got our streets safely back without ASBOs. We had nothing else in the tool box we could use – ASBOs really are the most powerful way forward to reduce the serious anti-social behaviour that blights neighbourhoods.'

Despite needing a police escort home after the trial because of fear of reprisals, Lynda added: 'The community is now carrying a badge of honour and we will carry on applying for more ASBOs. This sends a big message out to these girls who are working on the streets that we will not allow our neighbourhood to be abducted by aggressive, drug-fuelled individuals.'

Michelle Thomas, Cardiff

Gangs of youths were destroying Michelle's formerly quiet residential neighbourhood with nuisance including playing football when drunk and hitting the ball against cars and houses, playing loud music, urinating in front gardens and violent behaviour.

Michelle worked with the Cardiff ASB unit to keep diaries of incidents that took place to provide evidence, even though other local residents were too afraid of repercussions to act.

A total of eight ASBOs were secured and they have made a huge difference to the community. Michelle said: 'ASBOs are not a badge of honour in my street, they have made a world of difference.'

Although some of the ASBOs were breached initially, the swift action taken by the local services to follow this up means that behaviour has changed and the perpetrators know there will be serious repercussions if they continue to cause problems.

⇨ The above information is reprinted with kind permission from the Home Office. Visit www.respect.gov.uk for more information.

© Crown copyright

Prison sentences 'too soft'

Prison sentences are too lenient, say young people on HeadsUp forum

HeadsUp is the Hansard Society's innovative website where under-18s debate politics and political issues with legislators and other young people. The most recent debate discussed 'Crime in Britain: How big is the problem?' There were four main strands:

⇨ The police – do they treat young people fairly?
⇨ The media – does the media criminalise young people?
⇨ Law, punishment and justice – is prison enough to prevent re-offending?
⇨ Your community – do you feel safe?

Almost all forum users who commented felt that prison sentences are too lenient and some forum users commented that they felt a life sentence should mean the rest of the person's life is spent in jail:

I think that if someone gets a life imprisonment then they should spend the rest of their life in jail...People who commit less serious crimes often spend the same time in prison as someone who has committed a murder.

Many young people on the forum also thought that bringing back capital punishment was a good idea to deter people from committing crimes:

Punishment should be a deterrent, and I think that the ultimate deterrent is execution. Who would commit rape with the thought that would die if they were caught?

Other key points were:

⇨ Some suggested that, in their experience, the police deal with black and white teenagers differently;
⇨ Some were worried that older people who have little contact with younger people would believe the negative stereotypes portrayed in the media;
⇨ Many thought that the age of criminality was too high and that children know right and wrong much earlier;
⇨ Although some computer games and films glamorise violence, the film or games' level of realism and the background of the person using the game were also an influence on them when committing crime.

27 March 2009

⇨ The above information is reprinted with kind permission from the Hansard Society. Visit www.hansardsociety.org.uk for more information on this and other related topics.

© Hansard Society

More knife crime offenders jailed

More criminals are being jailed for carrying a knife and the number of offences dealt with involving knives has fallen, according to new statistics published by the Ministry of Justice today

The statistics also show that offenders caught carrying a knife are receiving longer prison sentences and fewer cautions.

Between January and March 2009 the statistics show a fall of seven per cent in the total number of offences involving possession of a knife or other offensive weapon dealt with to 6,477 from 6,931, compared to the same period in 2008. This fall increases to 15 per cent for youths aged between 10 and 17.

Statistics show that offenders caught carrying a knife are receiving longer prison sentences and fewer cautions

---

The number of prisoners serving a sentence for possession of an offensive weapon increased by nearly half again (44 per cent) between the first quarter of 2008 and the same period in 2009.

The figures show:

More offenders are being sent to jail

The proportion of immediate custodial terms given for possessing a knife or offensive weapon increased from 17 per cent of all sentences to one in five (20 per cent) between the first quarter of 2008 and the same period in 2009. The number of offences resulting in immediate custody rose 13 per cent from 1,167 to 1,320 during the same period.

Fewer offences are being dealt with

The number of cautions or sentences given to youths decreased by 15 per cent between the first quarter of 2009

and the same quarter in 2008 (from 1,591 to 1,359). For all age groups the number of cautions and sentences handed down decreased by seven per cent from 6,931 to 6,477 between the two periods.

Longer sentences are being handed down

The average immediate custodial sentence has risen by a third (33 per cent – from 139 days in the first quarter of 2008 to 185 days in the same period of 2009).

Tougher community sentences are being used more often

The proportion of community sentences given increased from 29 per cent to 33 per cent, while the number of offences resulting in community sentences rose nine per cent (from 1,977 in the first quarter of 2008 to 2,161 in the same period of 2009). These can include tough and visible Community Payback where offenders are required to undertake demanding physical work to pay back to the communities they have harmed.

Fewer cautions are being issued. The proportion of cautions for carrying a knife fell from 35 per cent to 25 per cent between the first quarter of 2008 and the same period this year. The number fell 33 per cent during the same time span (2,394 in the first quarter of 2008 compared to 1,599 in the same period of 2009).

More criminals are being jailed for carrying a knife and the number of offences dealt with involving knives has fallen

Justice Minister Maria Eagle said:

'These statistics show tougher penalties are being imposed by courts – which means more prison sentences and fewer cautions are being handed down.

'The government's rigorous stance on knife crime is clearly working – we have clamped down on criminals who carry knives, and anyone aged 16 or over caught in possession of a knife can now expect to be prosecuted on the first offence. More stringent penalties are being implemented by the courts, in line with Court of Appeal guidance.

'This progress is both positive and necessary, but we must work even harder to rid our streets of the scourge of knife crime. We will work with the police and the judiciary to ensure those who are caught with a knife are prosecuted and face a tough and visible punishment.

'And as the Lord Chief Justice, Lord Judge, spelt out, if you are caught carrying a knife the consequences are serious – there is a very good chance you could end up in prison.'

Policing Minister David Hanson said:

'These latest figures showing more people going to jail for carrying knives and for longer are very encouraging.

'The government is taking targeted action to tackle knife crime, particularly when it comes to young people. Between June 2008 and March 2009, forces in the ten original Tackling Knives Action Programme areas took more than 3,500 knives off the streets – each of which had the potential to inflict a serious or fatal injury. But we have always made clear that tough police enforcement is just one element of our strategy to deal with knife crime. It also includes ongoing work on education, prevention and prosecution to directly address the causes of knife crime.

'By continuing this targeted programme of action and extending the remit to include 13 to 24 year olds we have made it clear that we are committed to tackling the core minority of young people who persist in committing serious violence and working hard to make people feel safe in their communities.'

A fuller breakdown of the *Knife Crime Sentencing Quarterly Brief January to March 2009 England and Wales*, published by the Ministry of Justice, follows.

Offences by adults

There were 5,115 offences by adults dealt with in the first quarter of 2009 compared to 5,340 in the same period of 2008.

Of these there was a 15 per cent increase in the number which resulted in an immediate custodial sentence (1,234 compared to 1,074 in the same period in 2008). The proportion of immediate custodial sentences for carrying a knife increased from 20 per cent to 24 per cent.

Offences by 10 to 17 year olds

There were 1,359 offences by youths dealt with in the first quarter of 2009 compared to 1,591 in the same period of 2008.

The number of offences resulting in community sentences went up by seven per cent from 679 in the first quarter of 2008 to 725 in the same period of 2009. The proportion of community sentences as a part of all sentences increased from 43 per cent to 53 per cent.

11 June 2009

⇨ Information from the Ministry of Justice. Visit www.justice.gov.uk for more information.

© Crown copyright

Prison – why should I care?

Information from the Prison Reform Trust

How many people are in prison?

On 3 August 2007, there were 80,319 people in jail in England and Wales. Our rate is far higher then our European neighbours – in fact, it is now the highest imprisonment rate in Western Europe. It outstrips Saudi Arabia, Rwanda, China and Myanmar (Burma).

Why should that concern me?

Because, although when they are locked up they can't commit crime, most prisoners come out of jail and re-offend. Crime committed by ex-prisoners costs the taxpayer £11 billion. Nearly three-quarters of all young offenders and two-thirds of adults come out of jail and are re-convicted within two years. For certain crimes the rate is even higher – nearly 90 per cent of young male shoplifters are re-convicted within two years of release. It costs the country £40,992 to send each prisoner to jail for one year.

Why isn't prison stopping re-offending?

Prisoners go into jail with complex problems including drug addiction, unemployment and homelessness, which may have contributed to their offending. Nearly three-quarters have two or more mental disorders and most have no qualifications.

While there are some excellent schemes in prison which tackle these problems, overcrowding means that prisons are less able to provide education, training and rehabilitation work which stops prisoners re-offending when they are released. Two-thirds of prisons are overcrowded.

If overcrowding is a problem, why don't we just build more prisons?

Building new prisons has not solved overcrowding. In the last ten years 13 new prisons have been opened. By the end of May 2003, nine of these were overcrowded.

Is it true to say that people go in to prison bad and come out worse?

In many cases, yes – especially for those serving short custodial sentences. Prison does not generally make people take responsibility for themselves or face up to what they have done, but gives them the chance to swap criminal contacts and skills with other convicts. It can also mean them losing their job, home and family ties, meaning they are more likely to re-offend when they get out.

OK – prison isn't stopping crime. So what is?

It's been proven that programmes that punish non-violent offenders in the community can cut re-offending

rates by up to 53 per cent. These programmes are not a soft option. They work because they instil a sense of discipline and responsibility in offenders, making them face up to the damage they have caused, and in some cases compensating their victims. They also tackle the causes of crime such as drug addiction, unemployment and lack of education.

Isn't it better to stop crime before it starts?

Yes – and crime diversion schemes which stop young people becoming criminals in the first place are having a dramatic effect in reducing crime rates.

If community punishments are so great why aren't they used more often?

Contrary to popular belief, sentences have become much harsher over the last few years. Offenders who would have received a community penalty ten years ago are now more likely to receive a prison sentence. A first-time burglar is nearly twice as likely to go to jail today as eight years ago. Probation services are also over-stretched and under-funded.

⇨ The above information is reprinted with kind permission from the Prison Reform Trust. Visit www. prisonreformtrust.org.uk for more.

© Prison Reform Trust

KEY FACTS

⇨ Teenage killings in London have risen from 15 in 2006 to 27 in 2007, and stood at 21 halfway through 2008. (page 1)

⇨ According to the British Crime Survey (a big annual survey of experience of crime involving about 40,000 respondents), overall crime rates have fallen by around 40 per cent over the past decade. Violent crime has, however, failed to fall as quickly as other crime. (page 2)

⇨ Young men aged between 16 and 24 have the highest risk of being a victim of crime – 13 per cent (British Crime Survey 2007-08). (page 4)

⇨ 7% of men have a high level of worry about violent crime, compared with 19% of women. (page 6)

⇨ Carrying a knife could make you liable to a fine of up to £1,000, or a maximum of four years' imprisonment. If it's used to injure or threaten someone the penalties are more severe. (page 7)

⇨ Up to 50,000 young people are gang members. (page 9)

⇨ A study found that the six per cent of people self-reporting as gang members were responsible for over a fifth of all core offences and 40 per cent of all burglaries. (page 10)

⇨ 55% of young people surveyed as part of an NCB report strongly agreed and 33% agreed that the media should cover more positive stories about young people. (page 11)

⇨ Of 1,001 young people polled by the Barrow Cadbury Trust, 83% said that getting work experience and having good job opportunities is a key factor in helping young people move away from crime. (page 12)

⇨ There does not seem to be any boundary between young people socialising together in public spaces and 'gang' activity – causing groups of young people to be viewed as automatically suspicious. (page 14)

⇨ More than one in six of those aged 8 to 17 say they believe knife crime is a problem in their area – and this more than doubles to 36 per cent of young people from London. (page 15)

⇨ Youth courts deal with charges against young people aged 10-17. Those aged 10-13 are classified as 'children', 14-17 year olds as 'young persons'. Children under the age of 10 are deemed by law to be incapable of being guilty of a crime. (page 16)

⇨ The public wrongly attributes a large proportion of offending to young people or believes that youth offending has rapidly escalated. (page 21)

⇨ When asked to what extent they agreed or disagreed that children are increasingly a danger to each other and to adults, 37% of those surveyed said that they agreed. 12% strongly agreed. (page 22)

⇨ Better parenting is the top thing (58%) the public say would do most to reduce crime and 58% of the public think that Friday night is the most important time for youth facilities to be available. (page 23)

⇨ 68% of crimes are punished with a fine. 13% of offences receive a community sentence. Only 7% receive a prison sentence. (page 24)

⇨ In 2007, 162,648 people started court orders in the community, the highest ever recorded number. It represents a 36 per cent increase in the decade since 1997. The orders include both community sentences and Suspended Sentence Orders. (page 28)

⇨ Gun crime represents only 0.4% of all recorded crime in England and Wales. (page 29)

⇨ Police forces in England and Wales will receive more than 6,000 new Tasers, the Home Secretary announced recently. (page 32)

⇨ According to an exclusive YouGov poll commissioned by the CSJ working group, 76 per cent of people think that the police are intervening 'too little' against anti-social behaviour. (page 33)

⇨ If you are under 17, you should usually not be interviewed by the police without a parent or appropriate adult present (an appropriate adult is someone who knows you, such as an adult friend or teacher). (page 35)

⇨ Between January and March 2009 the statistics show a fall of seven per cent in the total number of offences involving possession of a knife or other offensive weapon dealt with to 6,477 from 6,931, compared to the same period in 2008. This fall increases to 15 per cent for youths aged between 10 and 17. (page 38)

⇨ On 3 August 2007, there were 80,319 people in jail in England and Wales. Our rate is far higher then our European neighbours – in fact, it is now the highest imprisonment rate in Western Europe. It outstrips Saudi Arabia, Rwanda, China and Myanmar (Burma). (page 39)

GLOSSARY

Age of criminal responsibility
In England, Wales and Northern Ireland, a child has to be 10 before they can be found guilty of committing a crime. The age was lowered from 14 to 10 in 1998 and is lower than in many other countries. Children under the age of 10 lack capacity to commit a crime: the legal term for this rule is *doli incapax*.
In Scotland, the age of criminal responsibility is eight – one of the lowest in Europe.

ASBO
ASBO stands for Anti-Social Behaviour Order. It is a civil order against behaviour which causes 'alarm, harassment or distress'. It can cover things such as graffiti, shoplifting or frequently playing loud music. ASBOs aim to protect the public against further anti-social behaviour from an individual rather than punish the person.

CCTV
Closed circuit television. These are mounted cameras which broadcast a live image to a television screen, which can then be monitored and recorded. They are used primarily for security purposes. With an estimated 4.2 million cameras in operation, the UK has more CCTV monitoring than any other country.

Crime
Crime may be defined as an act or omission prohibited or punished by law. A 'criminal offence' includes any infringement of the criminal law, from murder to riding a bicycle without lights. What is classified as a crime is supposed to reflect the values of society and to reinforce those values. If an act is regarded as harmful to society or its citizens, it is often, but not always, classified as a criminal offence.

Custody
In criminal terminology, being 'in custody' refers to someone being held in spite of their wishes, either by the police while awaiting trial (police custody), or, having received a custodial punishment, in a prison or other secure accommodation.

Non-custodial sentence
A punishment which does not require someone convicted of a crime to be held in custody, in prison or another closed institution. Community service, restraining orders and fines are all types of non-custodial punishment.

Reoffending rate
The rate at which a person, having been convicted of a crime and punished, will then go on to commit another crime (implying that the punishment was ineffectual as a crime deterrent).

Reparation
Reparation is a practical way for an offender to pay back for the harm caused when an offence was committed, either by directly repairing the harm or through constructive work to help the local community. The victim is usually consulted about what should be done.

Restorative justice
This usually involves a conference or meeting where the offender sits down with the victim, family members, and possibly other people from the community or people related to the crime. This means they do not have to make a court appearance. The purpose of the meeting is to discuss the offending behaviour and come up with ways for the person to 'repay' the victim or community for their crime.

Sentence
The punishment given by the judge to an individual who has been found guilty of a crime at the end of a criminal trial. This generally takes the form of a fine, a community punishment, a discharge or a period of imprisonment.

Stop and search
In England and Wales, the police have the power to stop members of the public and ask them what they are doing, where they are going, what they are carrying etc. They may also search the person if they are not happy with their response to the questions.

Taser
A 'stun gun' which can give a powerful electric shock, causing a victim to temporarily lose control of their muscles. It is an offence for a member of the public to possess a Taser, but they are issued to armed police as a 'less lethal' weapon than firearms.

Victim personal statement
This allows a crime victim to explain more about the impact of the crime on them personally. It can then be used by the judge or magistrate to help them decide on an appropriate sentence for the offender.

Youth courts
These deal with charges against young people aged 10 to 17. Those aged 10 to 13 are classified as 'children', those aged 14 to 17 as 'young persons'.

Young offenders
A young person who commits a crime between the age of criminal responsibility (10 in England and Wales) and their 18th birthday is classed as a juvenile offender. Between the ages of 18 and 20 (i.e. up to their 21st birthday), they are classed as young offenders.

INDEX

absolute discharge 17, 25
acceptable behaviour contracts (ABCs) 8
action plan orders 17
age of criminal responsibility 19
airguns and the law 7
anti-social behaviour 8
Anti-Social Behaviour Orders (ASBOs) 8, 18, 25, 36-7
arrest, your rights 35-6
ASBOs (Anti-Social Behaviour Orders) 8, 18, 25, 36-7
attendance centre orders 17, 26

bail 36
binding over 18

cautions 36
CCTV and anti-social behaviour 8
charge sheets 36
child safety orders 18
community punishments 17, 24, 25-6, 27-9
    community orders 24, 25-6
    community punishment orders 17
    community rehabilitation orders 17
    and knife crime 38
compensation orders 17, 25
conditional discharge 17, 25
crime levels 20
criminal responsibility, age of 19
curfew orders 17, 25

deferred sentences 18
detention and training orders 17-18
discharge 17, 24-5
DNA database 31-2
drug rehabilitation 26
drug treatment and testing orders 18

education and social breakdown 4
Engaging Communities in Fighting Crime review 23
ephebiphobia (fear of young people) 22

family breakdown 2
family group conferencing 31
fear of crime 2, 6, 20-21
fear of young people 3, 22
fines 17, 24
fingerprints 36
fixed penalty notices 8, 25

Gang Activity Desistance Orders (GADOs) 9
gangs 9-10, 12-14
    dealing with 9-10, 14
    definition 10
    signs of membership 12-13
gun crime 15-16, 29-30
    young people's concerns 15-16

guns and the law 7

high-visibility jackets for offenders 28-9

jail *see* prison

knife crime 15-16, 29-30
    sentencing 38-9
    statistics 38, 39
    young people's concerns 15-16
knives and the law 7

law and weapons 7, 30
legal advice on arrest 35

male violence, attitudes to 5
managing offenders 26
media influence on attitudes to crime 3-4

National Offender Management Service (NOMS) 26

parenting orders 18
penalty notices 8, 25
    penalty notice for disorder 8
police, young people's attitudes to 15-16
policing 33-4
powers of dispersal 8
prison 39
prison sentences 25, 37
    for knife crime 38
public attitudes to crime 6, 23
public perceptions
    of social problems 1-4
    of youth crime 3, 20-21

questioning by police 35

referral orders 17, 31
reparation orders 17, 31
Respect campaign 8
restorative conferencing 31
restorative justice 31
rights on arrest 35-6

sentencing 24-6
    community sentencing 24, 25-9
    knife crime 38-9
    youth courts 17-18
sex offenders notification 18
sexual offences prevention order 18
social pessimism 1-4
stop and search 34
street crime 4-5
street fighting 5
supervision orders 17, 26

suspended sentence orders 26

Tasers 31-2
teenage gangs *see* gangs

victim-offender mediation 31
violent street crime 4-5

weapons
  and crime 15-16, 29-30
  and the law 7, 30
  and sentences 38-9

young offenders 11-12
young people
  attitudes to police 15-16
  concerns over gun and knife crime 15-16
  fear of 3, 22
  gang membership 12-14
  improving profile of 21
youth courts 16-18
youth crime 9-22
  public perceptions 3, 20-21
  trends 20
youth justice 16-18

Additional Resources

Other Issues titles

If you are interested in researching further some of the issues raised in *Crime in the UK*, you may like to read the following titles in the **Issues** series:

⇨ Vol. 179 *Tackling Child Abuse* (ISBN 978 1 86168 503 2)

⇨ Vol. 175 *Citizenship and Participation* (ISBN 978 1 86168 489 9)

⇨ Vol. 174 *Selling Sex* (ISBN 978 1 86168 488 2)

⇨ Vol. 172 *Racial and Ethnic Discrimination* (ISBN 978 1 86168 486 8)

⇨ Vol. 168 *Privacy and Surveillance* (ISBN 978 1 86168 472 1)

⇨ Vol. 167 *Our Human Rights* (ISBN 978 1 86168 471 4)

⇨ Vol. 165 *Bullying Issues* (ISBN 978 1 86168 469 1)

⇨ Vol. 163 *Drugs in the UK* (ISBN 978 1 86168 456 1)

⇨ Vol. 160 *Poverty and Exclusion* (ISBN 978 1 86168 453 0)

⇨ Vol. 155 *Domestic Abuse* (ISBN 978 1 86168 442 4)

⇨ Vol. 147 *The Terrorism Problem* (ISBN 978 1 86168 420 2)

For more information about these titles, visit our website at www.independence.co.uk/publicationslist

Useful organisations

You may find the websites of the following organisations useful for further research:

⇨ **11 MILLION:** www.11million.org.uk

⇨ **Centre for Crime and Justice Studies:** www.crimeandjustice.org.uk

⇨ **Centre for Social Justice:** www.centreforsocialjustice.org.uk

⇨ **Criminal Justice System:** www.cjsonline.gov.uk

⇨ **Department for Children, Schools and Families:** www.dcsf.gov.uk

⇨ **Directgov:** www.direct.gov.uk

⇨ **Economic and Social Research Council:** www.esrcsocietytoday.ac.uk

⇨ **Home Office:** www.homeoffice.gov.uk

⇨ **Ipsos MORI:** www.ipsos-mori.com

⇨ **Local Government Association:** www.lga.gov.uk

⇨ **Ministry of Justice:** www.justice.gov.uk

⇨ **National Foundation for Educational Research:** www.nfer.ac.uk

⇨ **Policy Exchange:** www.policyexchange.org.uk

⇨ **Prisoners' Families Helpline:** www.prisonersfamilieshelpline.org.uk

⇨ **Prison Reform Trust:** www.prisonreformtrust.org.uk

⇨ **Runnymede Trust:** www.runnymedetrust.org

⇨ **TheSite:** www.thesite.org

⇨ **YouGov:** www.yougov.com

⇨ **Youth Justice Board:** www.yjb.gov.uk

ACKNOWLEDGEMENTS

The publisher is grateful for permission to reproduce the following material.

While every care has been taken to trace and acknowledge copyright, the publisher tenders its apology for any accidental infringement or where copyright has proved untraceable. The publisher would be pleased to come to a suitable arrangement in any such case with the rightful owner.

Chapter One: Crime and Violence
Does Britain need fixing?, © Ipsos MORI, *Violence in street crime*, © Economic and Social Research Council, *The right to fight?*, © Economic and Social Research Council, *Fear of crime or anxiety about a changing society?*, © Economic and Social Research Council, *Weapons and the law*, © TheSite, *Anti-social behaviour*, © Crown copyright is reproduced with the permission of Her Majesty's Stationery Office.

Chapter Two: Youth Crime
Police 'should break up gangs', © Centre for Social Justice, *Coping with kidulthood*, © Barrow Cadbury Trust, *Gang membership*, © Crown copyright is reproduced with the permission of Her Majesty's Stationery Office, *Get rid of 'gangs'*, © Runnymede Trust, *Gun and knife crime survey*, © 11 MILLION, *Youth justice*, © Prisoners' Families Helpline, *Too young to be a criminal*, © Guardian News & Media Ltd 2009, *Young people, crime and public perceptions*, © Local Government Association/NFER, *The fear of young people damages us all*, © Telegraph Media Group Limited (2009).

Chapter Three: Dealing with Crime
Engaging communities in fighting crime, © Crown copyright is reproduced with the permission of Her Majesty's Stationery Office, *Crime, sentencing and your community*, © Criminal Justice System, *Community sentencing*, © Crown copyright is reproduced with the permission of Her Majesty's Stationery Office, *Going ballistic*, © Policy Exchange, *Restorative justice*, © Youth Justice Board for England and Wales, *The danger of Tasers*, © Guardian News & Media Ltd 2009, *Thousands of new Tasers for police*, © Crown copyright is reproduced with the permission of Her Majesty's Stationery Office, *'Reclaim the streets' plea by new think-tank report*, © Centre for Social Justice, *Stop and search*, © Hansard Society, *Rights on arrest*, © TheSite, *How ASBOs help*, © Crown copyright is reproduced with the permission of Her Majesty's Stationery Office, *Prison sentences 'too soft'*, © Hansard Society, *More knife crime offenders jailed*, © Crown copyright is reproduced with the permission of Her Majesty's Stationery Office, *Prison – why should I care?*, © Prison Reform Trust.

Photographs
Stock Xchng: pages 3 (whirlybird); 9 (Gabriella Fabbri); 12 (Mario Alberto Magallanes Trejo); 29 (G Schouten de Jel); 37 (Elena Gorgievska); 38 (Maria Li).
Wikimedia Commons: page 32 (Junglecat).

Illustrations
Pages 1, 15, 27: Simon Kneebone; pages 5, 19, 33: Angelo Madrid; pages 10, 18: Bev Aisbett; pages 12, 23, 30, 35: Don Hatcher.

And with thanks to the team: Mary Chapman, Sandra Dennis, Claire Owen and Jan Sunderland.

Lisa Firth
Cambridge
September, 2009